HOW
SEX
WORKS

KT-159-725

HOW
SEX
WORKS

Elizabeth Fenwick
& Richard Walker

BCA

LONDON   NEW YORK   SYDNEY   TORONTO

A DORLING KINDERSLEY BOOK

Project editor Charyn Jones
Art editor Ursula Dawson
Deputy editorial director Daphne Razazan
Managing art editor Derek Coombes

This edition published 1994 by BCA by arrangement
with Dorling Kindersley Publishers Limited,
9 Henrietta Street, London WC2E 8PS
Copyright © 1994 Dorling Kindersley Limited,
London
Text copyright © 1994 Elizabeth Fenwick and
Richard Walker

All rights reserved. No part of this publication may
be reproduced, stored in a retrieval system,
or transmitted in any form or by any means,
electronic, mechanical, photocopying, recording, or
otherwise, without the prior written permission of
the copyright owner.

A CIP catalogue record for this book is available from
the British Library.

CN 8735

Reproduced by J. Film Process Pte, Thailand

Printed and bound in Great Britain
by Butler and Tanner Ltd

CONTENTS

BECOMING AN ADULT
Preparing yourself for relationships is crucial. Relationships don't just happen; making and sustaining them is a skill that everyone needs to learn.

INTRODUCTION

Sexuality is a natural and enjoyable part of life, and discovering your sexuality is a very important part of growing up. Experiencing these sexual feelings for the first time can be both difficult and confusing, and coping with the huge physical changes that take place as you move from childhood into adulthood is not easy either.

This book has been written to help you through that process. It is written for everyone aged 11 to 18 – boys and girls alike. We hope it provides straight answers to all your questions about both the physical and emotional aspects of sexuality and growing up.

Of course, you may feel you already know a lot about sex. Magazines, newspapers, television programmes, videos, and films seem full of it. People talk and joke about sex all the time, but sorting fact from fiction is not always so clear. Rumours and myths about sex abound. At the same time, many people find it embarrassing to talk openly and frankly about the subject. This can make it difficult to find answers to your questions – such as what is sex actually like, how do I decide when I am ready for sex, why does my best friend seem to be growing up so much faster than I am?

You may have all kinds of questions like these that you aren't comfortable discussing with anyone else. Some questions may be things you are quite worried about. Your body and your emotions change so fast during these teenage years that it can be an anxious and stressful time.

Sometimes you may wonder who you really are and what is happening to you. Everyone develops and grows up at such different rates so that "Am I normal?" is probably one of the most common questions you want to ask. Perhaps all your friends have started their periods before you have. Or maybe you feel awkward because your body is much more developed than your friends'. Or you could be feeling left out because everyone else seems to be talking about boyfriends and girlfriends and you're not sure whether you are even interested.

Learning to understand your sexual feelings is important, and deciding when you are ready for sex is another big issue. Sometimes the pressures to go further than you really want to can be strong. We hope this book will help to give you the confidence to go at your own pace and feel more in control. It should be your choice whether and when you decide to have sex and who with, and your right not to be rushed into sexual experience when you are not ready for it.

Like most human activities, sex has risks as well as pleasures. These are emotional as well as physical. There is a great deal of debate about increases in unplanned pregnancy and sexually transmitted infections. In this book we give you practical guidance on how to look after your own and your partner's health to avoid these risks.

Preparing yourself emotionally for relationships is crucial. Sexual feelings are strong, and the emotions that go with them can be equally powerful. This book deals with difficult feelings that everyone has to deal with at some time or another – the fear that someone you really like hasn't even noticed you, the pain when relationships break up, the worry about being the odd person out.

Clearly sex is about much more than the physical mechanics of sexual intercourse. Most people, whatever their age, enjoy sex when it is part of a caring relationship. But relationships don't just happen; making and sustaining relationships is a skill that everyone needs to learn.

The main aim of *How Sex Works* is to give you the knowledge that, together with your own experience, can enable you to understand better how to make your own decisions about sexuality and relationships. You are an individual with your own beliefs, views, and feelings about what is right and what is wrong. Part of growing up is about beginning to take responsibility for your own actions. We hope this book gives you the information to enable you to do this.

Doreen Massey
Director of the Family Planning Association, London

UNDERSTANDING YOUR BODY

Becoming a woman

Between the ages of 10 and 18, your body changes from that of a child to that of a woman. Your shape becomes more rounded and your weight almost doubles, as your waist narrows, and your breasts and hips develop.

The way you look is determined mainly by what you inherit from your parents. When your mother's egg and your father's sperm met during fertilization (*see page 70*), each was carrying a package of information consisting of thousands of genes that fused to provide a complete set of these pairs of genes. Each pair controls, or helps to control, one of your body's features such as skin colour, breast size, and height. A gene you inherit from your mother may be stronger than one from your father, or the other way round. For example, if you inherited a brown–eyed gene from your mother, and a blue–eyed gene from your father, you will probably have brown eyes, although the depth of colour will depend on other genes.

   Bodies don't differ just because of inherited characteristics, however. Lifestyle can make a difference as well. Some people eat more and their metabolism might mean that they put on weight; whereas others might eat a lot and stay the same weight. A healthy diet and exercise usually keep people fit and at their ideal weight.

PERSONAL HYGIENE

At around 12 or 13 sweat glands in your armpits start to work. Everyone sweats when they exercise or are excited or nervous, some more than others. Fresh sweat doesn't smell; its characteristic odour develops after a few hours. A daily bath or shower is important, and you might want to use a deodorant that stops the smell. If you sweat heavily, you could choose a deodorant combined with an anti-perspirant to reduce sweating. Whether you shave your armpits and legs or not is a matter of personal choice. Shaving and hair-removing creams can inflame the skin for a few hours so it is best not to apply a deodorant immediately after removing hair. Shaving is an easy way to remove unwanted hair, though hair removal creams (depilatories) and waxing have a longer-lasting effect.

GROWING UP
Until the age of 10 or 11, children grow steadily and slowly. But as puberty begins, growth accelerates so that within a year or two you will have outgrown your clothes. This growth spurt usually starts two years earlier in girls than it does in boys (*see page 20*). You then grow at a steady rate until, by the age of 18, you will have reached your adult

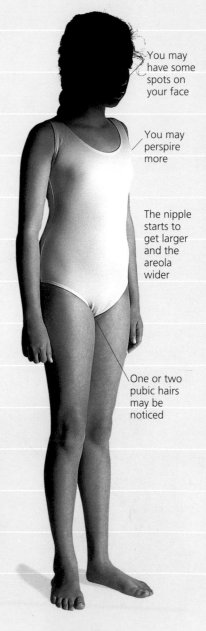

You may have some spots on your face

You may perspire more

The nipple starts to get larger and the areola wider

One or two pubic hairs may be noticed

12 years
Height: 137 cm/4 ft 6 in
Weight: 32 kg/70 lb

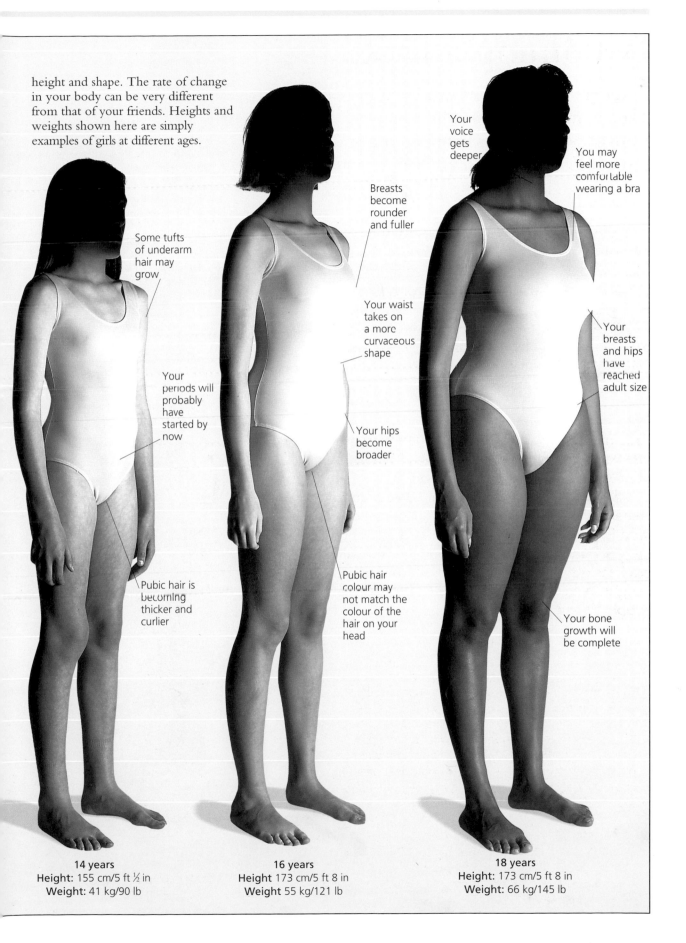

height and shape. The rate of change in your body can be very different from that of your friends. Heights and weights shown here are simply examples of girls at different ages.

Some tufts of underarm hair may grow

Your periods will probably have started by now

Pubic hair is becoming thicker and curlier

Breasts become rounder and fuller

Your waist takes on a more curvaceous shape

Your hips become broader

Pubic hair colour may not match the colour of the hair on your head

Your voice gets deeper

You may feel more comfortable wearing a bra

Your breasts and hips have reached adult size

Your bone growth will be complete

14 years
Height: 155 cm/5 ft ½ in
Weight: 41 kg/90 lb

16 years
Height 173 cm/5 ft 8 in
Weight 55 kg/121 lb

18 years
Height: 173 cm/5 ft 8 in
Weight: 66 kg/145 lb

A girl at puberty

Puberty is the time during which your body starts to change from a child's body to that of a woman. The changes do not begin at the same age for every girl, and the speed of change varies too.

The changes that occur during puberty happen because of the increase in the levels of the female sex hormones oestrogen and progesterone (*see page 16*). Puberty generally starts earlier in girls than in boys, usually around the age of 10 or 11, although it may begin before or after this age. As your body changes so will your feelings and attitudes (*see pages 30-31*).

You may notice that you grow more rapidly – this is known as a growth spurt. You may find yourself taller than many of the boys in your class. Your breasts start developing; strands of hair may grow on your pubic area (*see page 14*) and under your armpits; your hips, thighs, and breasts become more rounded. Your periods may begin (*see page 17*). There are changes to your internal organs too as they mature.

EATING WELL

The attitude that thin is beautiful is widespread in some cultures; in the western world it has been found that almost every woman diets at some time in her life. There is a real sense of achievement when the weight is lost. However, as you can see from inherited physical characteristics, not everyone grows up to look like a model in a magazine – thin and tall. For some girls, being thin becomes an obsession. Anorexia is an illness in which the sufferer sees herself as fat and continues to diet and perhaps exercise in an attempt to lose more weight. Even though she may be painfully thin, this will not be her perception of herself. Her weight may drop dramatically and her periods may stop. Occasionally anorexics starve themselves to death. Some develop bulimia, which is maintaining a normal weight by "binge eating" and then making themselves vomit the food up. People with these eating disorders need help, not just to get back to a healthier eating pattern, but because the disorder is usually a sign of underlying unhappiness. Both anorexia and bulimia are usually treated with expert counselling.

You will start to grow taller

Your skin secretes more oil

Perspiration glands become more active

The areola – the darker skin around the nipple – gets wider and darker

The hips start to become fleshier

Your thighs develop

A few pubic hairs may grow on the pubic area or around the labia

The internal organs also have a growth spurt during puberty

A GIRL AT PUBERTY

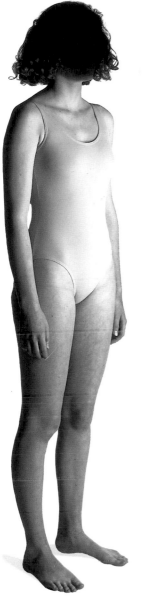

DIFFERENCES IN GROWTH

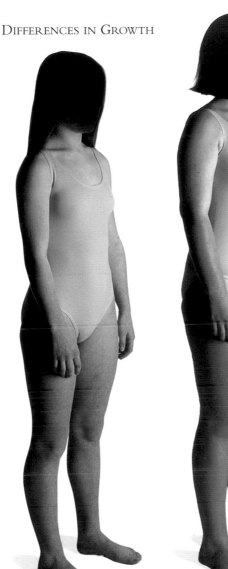

Height: 175 cm/5 ft 9 in
Weight: 57 kg/125 lb

Height: 155 cm/5 ft ½ in
Weight: 44 kg/97 lb

Height: 173 cm/5 ft 8 in
Weight: 67 kg/147 lb

Height: 162 cm/5 ft 3 in
Weight: 51 kg/112 lb

RATES OF GROWTH
Although changes to your body shape and size happen in a fairly orderly way, all girls develop at different rates. Some girls may experience a growth spurt at 11; others may not notice any difference in height until they are 13. It is usually at the time of this growth spurt that the body changes become noticeable and you have your first period. The girls pictured here are 13 and all aged within six months of one another.

QUESTIONS AND ANSWERS

I seem to get spots when I really want to look good. If I stopped eating chocolate would that help?
Shona, 14 years

Most nutritionists say that diet makes little difference because it is high levels of the sex hormones that lead to acne during adolescence. Washing your face regularly may help. You can buy skin washes and acne lotions from a pharmacist. If your spots are bad, it is worth seeing a doctor.

My breasts are small, but my friend says I still ought to wear a bra, or the muscles will get weak. Do I have to?
Sally, 13 years

Breasts have no muscles. Large breasts may droop without a bra, but if you have small breasts you won't need one, although you can wear one if you want to. The time to start wearing a bra is probably when you start to feel uncomfortable without one.

The female body

The reproductive system in the female body, including the eggs in the ovaries, is in place at birth. A signal in the brain at the onset of puberty starts the fertile stage of your life, causing one egg to be released every month until around the age of about 50.

Each month one egg matures and is released into one of the fallopian tubes. If sperm are there after recent sexual intercourse (*see pages 70-71*), the egg may be fertilized. The tubes lead to the uterus where the baby grows. The neck of the uterus is called the cervix. This has a mucus plug that thins at ovulation (when an egg is released), making it easier for sperm to swim through. The vagina is an elastic tube running to the opening at the vulva. It is quite separate from the urinary system, which has its own opening – the urethra.

The uterus is about the size and shape of a pear. It is the most muscular organ in the body and it is capable of huge expansion. It usually tilts forwards, almost at a right angle to the vagina. Its lower part, the cervix, opens into the vagina, and the tip of the cervix can just be felt at the top of the vagina.

During puberty (*see page 12*) the external sexual organs develop and mature. The mons pubis – the pad of fat covering the pubic bone – becomes fleshier and more prominent. Pubic hair grows on the labia and the mons pubis.

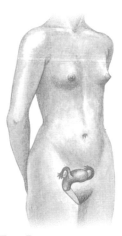

THE PELVIS
The reproductive organs lie in the pelvis (body cage) where they are protected. The uterus lies above and behind the bladder and in front of the rectum.

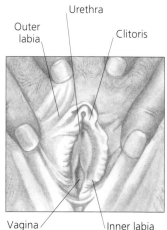

Outer labia · Urethra · Clitoris · Vagina · Inner labia

THE VULVA
Between two outer fleshy lips, or labia, on which the pubic hair grows, are two thinner and hairless inner labia. Between these are the clitoris, at the front, the opening of the urethra, in the middle, and the larger vaginal opening behind that.

THE STRUCTURE OF THE BREASTS

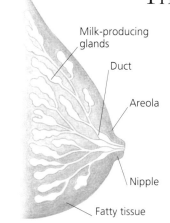

Milk-producing glands · Duct · Areola · Nipple · Fatty tissue

Breasts are made up of fatty tissue containing tiny milk-producing glands. All women have a similar number of glands, but some have more fatty tissue than others. This is why some breasts are larger than others. Ducts run from the glands to the surface of the nipple. The nipple is the most sensitive part of the breast. It is soft, but cold, and both touch and sexual arousal make it hard and erect. Around the nipple is the areola, an area of pink or brown skin, which darkens with age and pregnancy. During pregnancy the milk-producing ducts increase in preparation for lactation. They replace much of the fat that is normally in the breast. Milk is made inside the glands when a woman has had a baby. The milk travels through the ducts to the nipple as the baby sucks.

Fimbriae lie near the surface of the ovary and receive eggs

FROM OVARY TO UTERUS

At its upper end, the uterus opens out into the fallopian tubes, whose fringed ends lie near the surface of the ovaries. In this illustration, the fallopian tubes and ovaries are shown larger than life size; in reality, an ovary is about 3 cm (1¼ in) long, and the eggs in it are minute. The fallopian tube is about 1 mm (⅕ in) thick.

At birth, the ovaries contain about 400,000 eggs, or ova, in sacs called follicles. One egg is released each month. The empty follicle develops into the corpus luteum. Ovaries also produce the female sex hormones oestrogen and progesterone

The uterus is a hollow, pear-shaped, muscular organ. It is capable of huge expansion to accommodate a baby

The inside of a fallopian tube is no wider than the diameter of a human hair. Cells in the tubes sweep eggs to the uterus. If sperm are present, fertilization may take place in the tube

The cervix, the neck of the uterus, leads to the vagina. It is plugged with mucus with only a small hole to allow blood to pass through during periods. However, at ovulation the mucus thins making it easier for sperm to enter the uterus

Bladder

Clitoris

Urethra

Rectum

The vagina is about 8 cm (3 in) long, with ridged walls. These normally lie against each other, but because they are elastic they can open during intercourse and stretch in childbirth. In childhood, the vaginal opening is partially covered by a membrane called the hymen

QUESTIONS AND ANSWERS

If you're a virgin, is your vagina completely closed?
Rebecca, 14 years

A membrane called a hymen surrounds the vaginal opening. Only very rarely does it block the whole opening – there is normally a hole in it at least big enough to allow the menstrual blood to flow out. In some women, the hole is much larger. The hymen is eventually torn or stretched by vigorous exercise, using tampons, or sexual intercourse.

What happens to the eggs that don't get used?
Jan, 13 years

Out of the 400,000 eggs present in your ovaries at birth, probably only about 400 mature to be released at ovulation. The rest fail to mature and are reabsorbed into your body. The menopause occurs when there are no eggs to be released.

Someone told me that twins happen because of something in the man's or the woman's

system, and that they run in families. Is this true?
Adam, 14 years

Fraternal twins do tend to run in families. If a woman's ovaries shed two eggs at once and they are both fertilized, she will have fraternal twins. These twins are not identical and may be different sexes. Identical twins develop when one egg is fertilized by a single sperm and the egg divides to form two babies. These twins are the same sex and look alike.

The menstrual cycle

If an egg is not fertilized by sperm on its voyage down the fallopian tube, the lining of the uterus, which has prepared itself for the egg, is shed through the vagina. This monthly shedding of the lining of the uterus is called menstruation, or a period.

Periods are the sign that your hormones have stimulated your ovaries to begin releasing eggs. They also mean that you are physically able to have a baby. First periods usually begin between the ages of 11 and 14, but some girls start as early as nine and others not until they are 16.

The blood that comes out through the vagina is often scant at first, and for the first six months it may not be bright red but brownish. There may be just a trickle the first day, a heavier flow during the second and third day, then less and less until your discharge is back to normal on the fifth or sixth day. For the first two days, there may be some discomfort, with abdominal cramps. This is quite common.

Your cycle may be irregular for a while – periods may be missed – but after a few months, there will be a regular pattern. The average length of the menstrual cycle (from the first day of one period to the first day of the next) is 28 days, but all women have slightly different cycles.

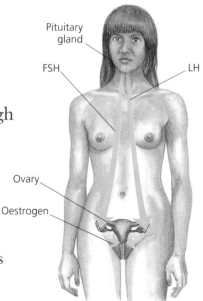

Pituitary gland

FSH

LH

Ovary

Oestrogen

HORMONAL CONTROL
The events of the menstrual cycle are controlled by hormones. Follicle-stimulating hormone (FSH) and luteinizing hormone (LH), released by the pituitary gland in the brain, are carried by the bloodstream to the ovary. Here they cause an egg to ripen and be released, and the ovary to release another two hormones, oestrogen and progesterone, that thicken the lining of the uterus, or endometrium.

DYSMENORRHOEA

This is the medical word for very painful periods. The lower abdominal pains are called cramps, and they feel as if something is pulling at your insides. Painkillers can help. Sometimes you may feel very ill, and you might even vomit. If your period pains are particularly severe, you should go to a doctor, who may prescribe a drug which will relieve the symptoms. Don't despair because dysmenorrhoea can be treated successfully. The pains usually get less as you get older or if you start to use the contraceptive pill. Exercise or yoga can also help relieve the discomfort.

QUESTIONS AND ANSWERS

Is it true you can't get pregnant before your periods have started?
Simone, 13 years

In theory you could, because they might be about to, but it is unlikely. Usually no egg is released during the first few menstrual cycles.

How do I know when I'm likely to start having my periods?
Alison, 14 years

Your period won't start until your growth spurt has begun and your breasts and pubic hair are growing. Starting early or late runs in families: if your mother started her periods late, you may, too. You may notice some whitish discharge for about a year before the bleeding begins.

Some girls at school get off physical education when they have their period. I like playing sport, should I miss it too?
Connie, 14 years

You can do anything during your period that you do at any other time. Exercise can even help to reduce cramps and it may make you feel better. Depression, irritability, spots, headaches, swollen or tender breasts, and stomach cramps are symptoms that some women get during their period. Whatever the symptom, you need to find a remedy that works for you. One of the best remedies for cramps is a hot water bottle. If necessary, take the recommended dose of a painkiller that is sold for menstrual pain.

THE MENSTRUAL CYCLE

Although the average length of the menstrual cycle is 28 days, the variation in the length of a cycle can be anything from 21 to 42 days. However long the menstrual cycle is in days, ovulation occurs 12 to 16 days *before* the beginning of the next period. If the egg is not fertilized, the uterine lining is shed through the vagina. During the cycle, the cervical mucus also changes. This can be used as an indication of ovulation (*see page 68*).

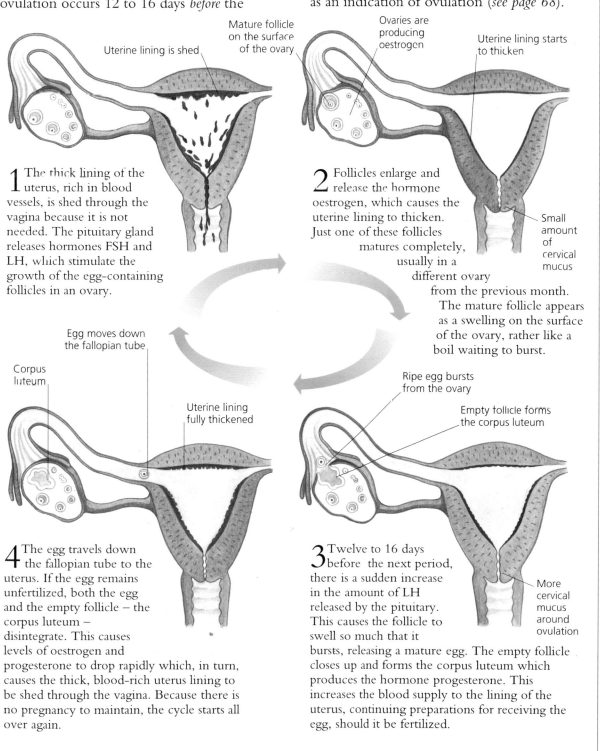

Uterine lining is shed

Mature follicle on the surface of the ovary

Ovaries are producing oestrogen

Uterine lining starts to thicken

1 The thick lining of the uterus, rich in blood vessels, is shed through the vagina because it is not needed. The pituitary gland releases hormones FSH and LH, which stimulate the growth of the egg-containing follicles in an ovary.

2 Follicles enlarge and release the hormone oestrogen, which causes the uterine lining to thicken. Just one of these follicles matures completely, usually in a different ovary from the previous month. The mature follicle appears as a swelling on the surface of the ovary, rather like a boil waiting to burst.

Small amount of cervical mucus

Egg moves down the fallopian tube

Corpus luteum

Uterine lining fully thickened

Ripe egg bursts from the ovary

Empty follicle forms the corpus luteum

4 The egg travels down the fallopian tube to the uterus. If the egg remains unfertilized, both the egg and the empty follicle – the corpus luteum – disintegrate. This causes levels of oestrogen and progesterone to drop rapidly which, in turn, causes the thick, blood-rich uterus lining to be shed through the vagina. Because there is no pregnancy to maintain, the cycle starts all over again.

3 Twelve to 16 days before the next period, there is a sudden increase in the amount of LH released by the pituitary. This causes the follicle to swell so much that it bursts, releasing a mature egg. The empty follicle closes up and forms the corpus luteum which produces the hormone progesterone. This increases the blood supply to the lining of the uterus, continuing preparations for receiving the egg, should it be fertilized.

More cervical mucus around ovulation

Your periods

No one knows quite why menstruation starts, but we do know that a gland in the brain triggers the process around 9 to 16 years, by releasing hormones. These in turn stimulate the ovaries to produce the female sex hormones which encourage the body to change.

For past generations of women menstruation has been an unmentionable, a time when women were seen as unclean. Today, with more open attitudes to sexuality, girls can feel excited and proud, although others may still experience negative feelings and feel frightened; many girls still start their periods without ever having been told what to expect.

Having a period is a completely normal part of a woman's life, and yet many girls feel embarrassed and uncomfortable during this time. This may depend upon how helpful and supportive your parents are. Girls often worry that they may smell, or that blood may leak onto their clothes, and everyone will know what is happening to them. Girl friends will understand these feelings, but boys may be insensitive and tease you. If you are unembarrassed and matter-of-fact about it, they may be too.

You might find it a good idea to keep a diary of your periods so that you can see how your personal cycle develops. Depending on how regular you are, you will be able to calculate what to expect and when to expect it.

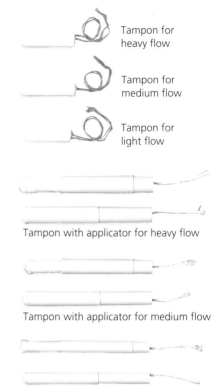

Tampon for heavy flow

Tampon for medium flow

Tampon for light flow

Tampon with applicator for heavy flow

Tampon with applicator for medium flow

Tampon with applicator for light flow

TAMPONS

A tampon is a tight roll of cotton wool with a string at one end. Tampons are available in different thicknesses to suit your rate of flow. If there are leaks, you can either use a higher absorbency tampon or change the tampon more often. You can't put a tampon in the wrong opening, and it cannot get lost inside.

PERSONAL HYGIENE

Good personal hygiene is particularly important during your period. Wash around the vagina, but not inside it – the lining is sensitive, and soap may sting. The vagina keeps itself clean; douches, sprays, and deodorants are all unnecessary. Scented bubble baths and bath oils may cause irritation. It is important to change tampons frequently – at least four times a day – to prevent the growth of bacteria in the vagina. This can lead to a condition called toxic shock syndrome (*see page 64*).

SANITARY TOWELS

Sanitary towels are soft cotton pads with one waterproof side. They are used to absorb menstrual blood and are worn outside the body, unlike tampons. Towels come in thicknesses suited to the rate of flow, which varies over the course of a period. They press-on to fit on the gusset of your knickers; some have wing shapes to hold them more firmly and provide for a heavier flow and prevent staining. Towels should be changed several times a day. Some women prefer towels when there is spotting rather than a steady flow and at night.

Panty liner with wings

Shaped panty liner

INSERTING A TAMPON

Tampons are worn inside the vagina, inserted with an applicator or with your finger. They are convenient for sports and can be worn during swimming. Low-absorbency tampons are useful when there is spotting rather than a steady flow.

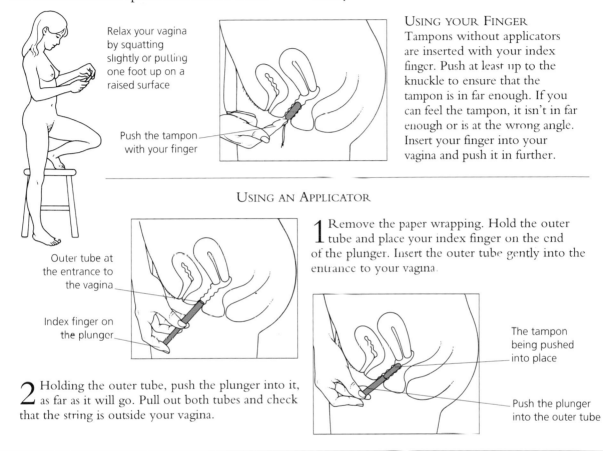

Relax your vagina by squatting slightly or pulling one foot up on a raised surface

Push the tampon with your finger

USING YOUR FINGER

Tampons without applicators are inserted with your index finger. Push at least up to the knuckle to ensure that the tampon is in far enough. If you can feel the tampon, it isn't in far enough or is at the wrong angle. Insert your finger into your vagina and push it in further.

USING AN APPLICATOR

Outer tube at the entrance to the vagina

Index finger on the plunger

1 Remove the paper wrapping. Hold the outer tube and place your index finger on the end of the plunger. Insert the outer tube gently into the entrance to your vagina.

The tampon being pushed into place

Push the plunger into the outer tube

2 Holding the outer tube, push the plunger into it, as far as it will go. Pull out both tubes and check that the string is outside your vagina.

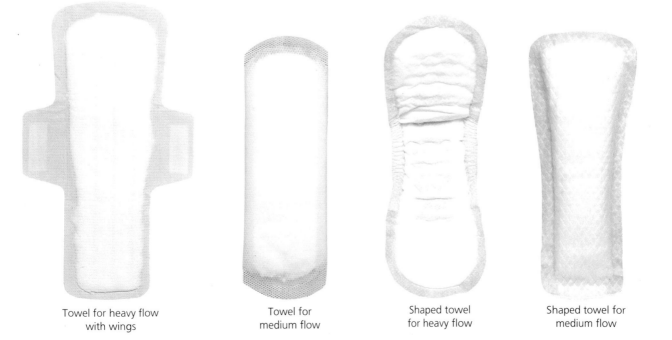

Towel for heavy flow with wings

Towel for medium flow

Shaped towel for heavy flow

Shaped towel for medium flow

Becoming a man

Between the ages of 13 and 18 your body changes from that of a child to that of a man. Your weight almost doubles, and your height increases. However, no two boys change in precisely the same way at the same age.

As you develop into a man you will grow body hair, and your voice will become deep. You may find this embarrassing, because one minute you may have a deep voice, and the next your voice will be high and squeaky. What you look like depends a lot on what your parents look like and the genes you inherit from them (*see page 10*). If your father has a lot of body hair, you probably will as well. Bodies also differ depending on the way they are treated – whether with a diet of nutritious food or junk food, for example.

Every boy is different, and physical changes in some boys may start at age 12 while other boys will develop even later. Many boys worry that they are developing too slowly or too quickly. It is easy to tease someone because they are bigger and hairier, or smaller and less hairy, than everyone else. However, everyone will eventually go through the same changes, although no two boys will look exactly the same.

GROWING UP
You will have reached your adult height by the age of 18. By your early twenties you will have reached your full height and breadth. If there are tall people in either

You may have some spots on your face

A few underarm hairs may appear

You may perspire more

One or two pubic hairs may be noticed

12 years
Height: 156 cm/5 ft 1 in
Weight: 45 kg/99 lb

QUESTIONS AND ANSWERS

My friends have started laughing about me and saying that I smell. What can I do?
William, 14 years

Many things about your body change as you grow up. One of these is that you start to sweat more, and that your sweat smells different. Take a bath or shower every day, and wear clean clothes and socks whenever possible. Use an anti-perspirant; you can buy these in supermarkets and pharmacies.

What should I do about the fluffy hair growing on my face?
Ben, 15 years

The first facial hair is easily, and safely, removed using soap and water, or shaving foam, and the sort of disposable razor that can be bought in supermarkets. It is not really thick enough yet to use an electric shaver.

My breasts have started to swell, and they are quite sore under the nipples. Am I going to change into a girl?
Adam, 15 years

This happens in quite a few boys of your age and is nothing to worry about. It is caused by the reaction to the sex hormones that are causing all the changes in your body, and it should not last more than a few months.

parent's family, you might be tall yourself. Heights and weights shown here are simply examples of boys at different ages.

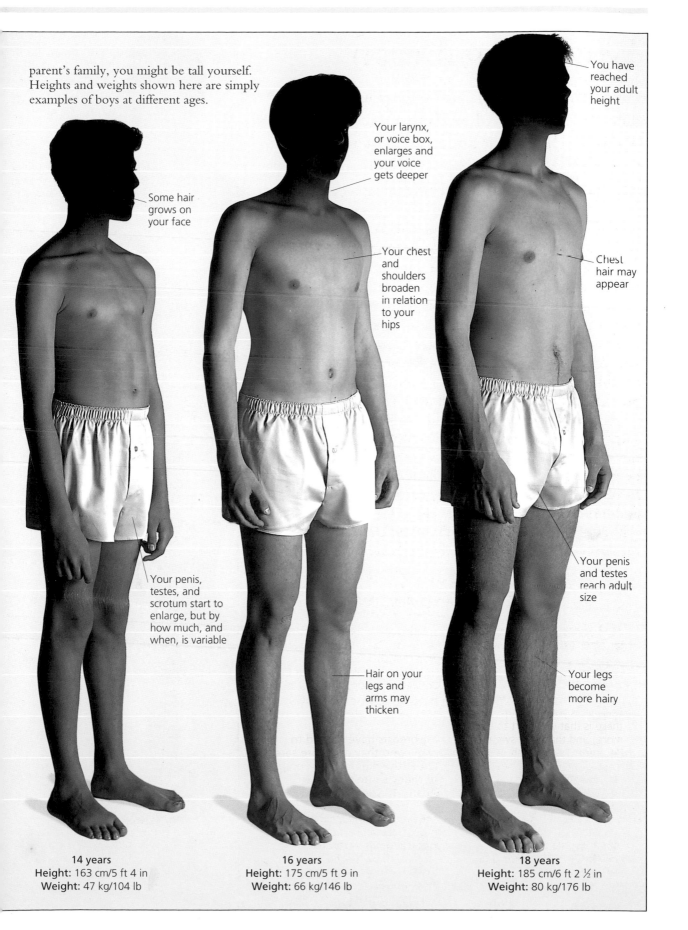

Some hair grows on your face

Your larynx, or voice box, enlarges and your voice gets deeper

Your chest and shoulders broaden in relation to your hips

You have reached your adult height

Chest hair may appear

Your penis, testes, and scrotum start to enlarge, but by how much, and when, is variable

Hair on your legs and arms may thicken

Your penis and testes reach adult size

Your legs become more hairy

14 years
Height: 163 cm/5 ft 4 in
Weight: 47 kg/104 lb

16 years
Height: 175 cm/5 ft 9 in
Weight: 66 kg/146 lb

18 years
Height: 185 cm/6 ft 2 ½ in
Weight: 80 kg/176 lb

A boy at puberty

Puberty is the time of life when a boy starts to become sexually mature. Your reproductive organs develop, and your testes start producing sperms. Your body begins a phase of growth and change in shape that will continue until the late teens.

Puberty is triggered by a hormone, released by the pituitary gland in the brain. This stimulates the testes to release the male sex hormone, testosterone, which controls the changes happening to your body. Puberty starts later in boys than girls, usually around the age of 14, although it may begin before or after this age. Puberty does not happen overnight. It forms part of the transition from boy to man called adolescence. As your body matures, you will find that your feelings and attitudes change as well (*see pages 30-31*).

THE MAJOR CHANGES

By the age of 13 or 14 you will probably notice some change. There may be differences in the age at which the different stages of change happen. First the testes start to grow. As they do so, the scrotum (the bag containing the testes) expands, hangs low and gets more wrinkly. The scrotum's skin gets redder in colour, if you have fair skin, or darker, if you have dark skin; it also becomes thicker. A few pubic hairs grow around the place where the penis joins the body, and some hair may grow under your armpits.

 The penis starts growing longer and thicker, and the skin colour also darkens. The testes and scrotum continue enlarging, and one testis, usually the left, hangs lower. Tiny bumps appear on the skin of the scrotum, and perhaps the penis, showing where hair may grow. Pubic hair will eventually spread upwards and to the sides, and become thicker and more curly. The body starts its growth spurt, getting larger and heavier, with broader shoulders and narrower hips.

 You will start to sweat more, and you may find that you need to wash more often and use deodorants and anti-perspirants to avoid body odours. Spots might appear, usually on the chin or nose, which is the area on the face where the skin secretes more oils.

Your skin secretes more oil

Perspiration glands become more active

Some hair growth under the arms

A few pubic hairs appear at the base of the penis

You will start to grow taller

A BOY AT PUBERTY

DIFFERENCES IN GROWTH

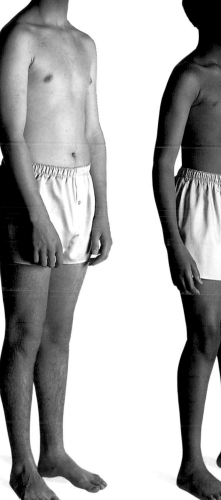

Height: 183 cm/6 ft ½ in
Weight: 70 kg/154 lb

Height: 167 cm/5 ft 6 in
Weight: 58 kg/128 lb

Height: 178 cm/5 ft 10 in
Weight: 76 kg/167 lb

Height: 175 cm/5 ft 9 in
Weight: 63 kg/139 lb

LOOKING AT DIFFERENCES
Everyone is different, both in the rate of the changes they experience, and in the shape and size they eventually reach at adulthood. This is your inheritance from your parents. You may feel gawky and unattractive, or smaller and less hairy than your friends – everyone has some feature that they are embarrassed about. All the boys pictured here are 15 or 16 years old and are all aged within six months of one another.

QUESTIONS AND ANSWERS

I've started getting spots. Why?
Jason, 14 years

Testosterone also makes the skin produce extra oils. Sometimes the glands in the skin that produce these oils get blocked, and you get spots. Keep your skin clean with an antibacterial soap, and don't pick the spots; otherwise you may get scarring. If they are really bad, you may have a condition called acne, and your doctor may be able to help.

How big should a penis be? My friends' all look much bigger than mine. It makes me really depressed.
Bobby, 15 years

Ask any male what part of his body he feels most unhappy about, and he will probably say the size of his penis, whatever age he is. A fully grown penis is usually between 8-10 cm (3-4 in) long when soft, and between 12-18 cm (5-7 in) long when it is erect, or stiff.

Male reproductive system

The male reproductive system isn't just a penis and testes that lie outside your body. Inside your body there is a system of ducts and glands that play an essential part in sperm production and delivery. Sperm are the male sex cells needed to make a baby.

From puberty to old age, millions of sperm are formed every day in the testes. It takes about 70 days for a sperm to be produced. Sperm can't develop properly at normal body temperature, so the testes hang outside the body, in the cooler scrotum. From the testis, sperm pass into a tube at the back of each testis – the epididymis – where the sperm mature. When a man ejaculates, muscle contractions squeeze the sperm along the sperm duct and into the urethra, passing on the way the openings of the seminal vesicles and the prostate gland. These produce seminal fluids, which mobilize the sperm and make up the bulk of the semen that is ejaculated from the penis.

The shaft of the penis contains spongy erectile tissue, which fills with blood during an erection. The head, or glans, is highly sensitive. Sperm are ejaculated from the penis along the urethra. This is normally a channel for urine, but muscles at the bladder entrance contract during erection, so that no urine enters the semen, and no semen enters the bladder. Any sperm that are not ejaculated are reabsorbed within a certain time into the man's body.

MALE HORMONE

Testosterone is the male sex hormone that is made in the testes, and is needed for sperm production. During puberty, it also:

- Enlarges the penis, testes, and scrotum, and increases their sensitivity.
- Promotes growth and increases muscle bulk in the body.
- Stimulates growth of facial and bodily hair.
- Deepens the voice.
- Increases both skin thickness and oily skin secretions, causing spots.
- Kick-starts sexual activity, increasing a boy's sex drive and interest.

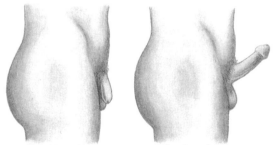

Flaccid penis   Erect penis

ERECTIONS AND SIZE DIFFERENCES
The penis hangs down, but during sexual arousal it becomes larger and points outwards and upwards, designed to deposit sperm in the vagina. Penises vary in size; size has nothing to do with masculinity, sexual performance, or pleasure.

CIRCUMCISION

All boys are born with a foreskin, a fold of skin that covers the glans of the penis. Sometimes the foreskin is cut away soon after birth, either as a religious rite, or in the belief that this is more hygienic, or it may be cut at a later age if it is tight (*page 52*). This operation is called a circumcision. Hygiene is not a problem with a foreskin if it is regularly pulled back and the secretions beneath it are washed away. Whether you have a foreskin or not will not affect your sexual health in the future.

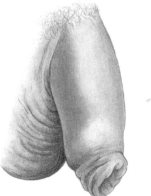
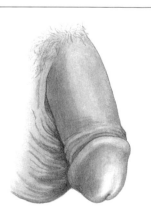

Uncircumcised penis   Circumcised penis

THE MALE REPRODUCTIVE ORGANS

The external organs are the penis and the testes. The testes hang in the scrotum, a pouch of skin behind the penis: the left usually hangs slightly lower than the right. During intercourse, semen is ejaculated from the penis into the woman's vagina to fertilize her eggs.

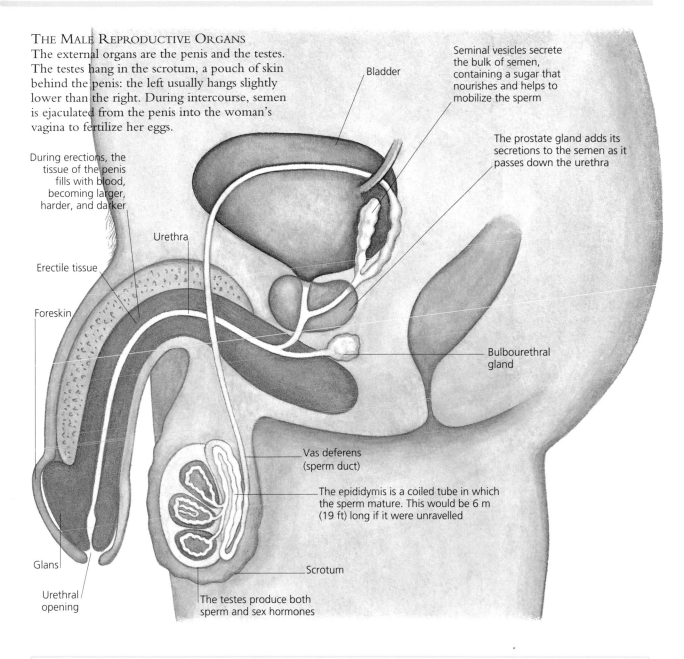

Seminal vesicles secrete the bulk of semen, containing a sugar that nourishes and helps to mobilize the sperm

Bladder

The prostate gland adds its secretions to the semen as it passes down the urethra

During erections, the tissue of the penis fills with blood, becoming larger, harder, and darker

Urethra

Erectile tissue

Foreskin

Bulbourethral gland

Glans

Urethral opening

Vas deferens (sperm duct)

The epididymis is a coiled tube in which the sperm mature. This would be 6 m (19 ft) long if it were unravelled

Scrotum

The testes produce both sperm and sex hormones

QUESTIONS AND ANSWERS

Why do I seem to wake up with an erection every morning? Is this normal?
Paul, 14 years

This happens to many boys and men. Erections can occur in dreams, whether or not the dream is sexual. If it is sexual, it may result in a "wet dream" (*page 27*). Often when you wake up, you may have an erection because your bladder is full.

Why do I keep having erections all the time, even when I'm not thinking about girls or anything?
Will, 14 years

Most boys have spontaneous erections, which are embarrassing if they happen at the wrong time or in the wrong place. They are caused by the raised levels of testosterone in the body and will stop as puberty passes. They do go away if you think about something else.

Is it true that wearing tight jeans can make a man infertile?
Joanna, 16 years

Anything that affects sperm production affects fertility. Tight jeans can raise the temperature of the scrotum, preventing sperm from developing properly. Sperm are produced all the time, however, so while wearing tight jeans may lower a man's fertility temporarily, it would not affect it in the future.

Your body's sensuality

As your body matures, you will become more aware of its sensitivity and sensuality. Discovering, exploring, and understanding your sensitivity can help you to enjoy your sex life to the full: sexual enjoyment involves the whole body, not just the sex organs.

> *I just love having my ear lobes kissed. It drives me wild and makes me feel tingly inside.*
>
> Annette, 16 years

WHAT IS MASTURBATION?

Masturbation means touching or rubbing your genitals or your partner's to give sexual pleasure, and usually to have an orgasm. Orgasm is a throbbing feeling that brings intense pleasure. For many people, masturbation is their first sexual experience. It is a harmless and natural way of enjoying sexuality on your own. It relieves the tension that results from sexual urges. It helps you to explore your body, discovering which sensations excite you – knowledge that you can share with a partner to show them how you like to be aroused. It will also help you to appreciate that sexual pleasure is not the simple mechanical exercise so often represented in the media. Good sexual relations take time and consideration.

Some people find out about masturbation from brothers, sisters, or friends, while others discover it on their own. By the late teens, the majority of boys and girls will have masturbated. Some people never feel a need to masturbate, and this is quite normal as well.

HOW PEOPLE MASTURBATE

There are no fixed ways to masturbate. Everyone does what pleases them. Most people have sexual fantasies *(see overleaf)* while they masturbate. Some people become aroused by looking at pornography.

Girls generally rub and stroke around and over the clitoris with their fingers, moving faster and faster until they have an orgasm. As sexual excitement rises, the vagina becomes moist. Girls can have several orgasms, one after the other. Stimulation of the clitoris is the main way that girls experience orgasm.

Most boys hold their penis and move their hand up and down to stimulate the glans; some boys rub just the glans, increasing the speed until they reach orgasm. The penis becomes limp after ejaculation.

Wet dreams happen to a boy during sleep – perhaps dreaming about something sexually exciting. You might become sexually aroused and ejaculate sperm in your sleep. You might wake up because the semen is cold on your skin or

WHO MASTURBATES?

Surveys show that by their late teens, about 90 percent of boys masturbate. The numbers for girls vary from as low as 60 percent to as high as 80 percent. Social attitudes and education may account for these differences: sexual double standards and the discredited idea that women shouldn't enjoy sex might make girls feel more guilty about masturbating than boys, and make some girls less likely than others to masturbate.

pyjamas. You might even be shocked because the dream was about a girl or boy who you would not normally think about in a sexual way. Wet dreams are quite normal and are one sign that you are becoming sexually mature, although not all boys have them. You may also experience spontaneous erections at unexpected times and even in public places.

Many girls also have dreams that make them sexually aroused, and sometimes they will have orgasms in their sleep. These are not really "wet" dreams, because girls don't ejaculate.

GUILT AND MYTHS ABOUT MASTURBATION

Many people feel guilty about masturbating. Small children find natural pleasure in touching their genitals, only to be told off by adults. This can lead to confusion and leave feelings of

I had my first orgasm while I was in the shower. Soaping myself down there felt really good, so I just kept going.
Martha, 15 years

I have really strange thoughts when I masturbate but I don't think I would ever do what I think about in real life.
Colin, 15 years

EROGENOUS ZONES

Your body is covered with touch and pressure sensors that, when touched or stroked, can make you feel sexually aroused and excited. These are known as erogenous zones. The genitals are usually the most sensitive zones on the body.

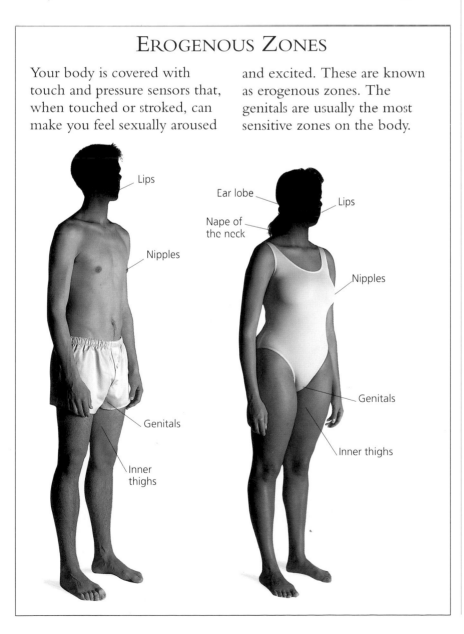

Lips

Ear lobe

Lips

Nape of the neck

Nipples

Nipples

Genitals

Genitals

Inner thighs

Inner thighs

The first time I had a wet dream, I thought there was something wrong with me. When it happened to my younger brother, he was really embarrassed because he thought he'd wet the bed, and I had to explain it all to him.

Brian, 18 years

guilt and shame about touching themselves. These guilt feelings can conflict with their sexual urges when they reach puberty and, later, when they become sexually active.

Your parents may not talk to you about masturbation, or they may discourage you. This is probably because of what their parents told them when they were young. Masturbation was once believed to cause poor health, loss of sight, paralysis, and madness, and boys and girls were punished for touching their genitals. These fears have been proved completely wrong, but even today, you may hear people say that masturbation makes you go blind, drives you mad, or wears out your sex organs. All myths of this kind are completely untrue and ought to be ignored.

SEXUAL FANTASIES

Most people have fantasies – or daydreams – at some time. You might imagine that you are a great athlete or singer or dream about what you will achieve. No one will ever know these thoughts, unless you tell them. Sexual fantasies are the same. It is normal to have sexual fantasies while you masturbate or at any other time. Some people worry because they fantasize about things they would never do in real life: you might imagine that you are having sex in public or with someone unexpected or watching others have sex. But a fantasy can stay just that and will add to your sexual enjoyment. However wild your fantasies are, you have nothing to worry about.

QUESTIONS AND ANSWERS

I'm in a football team. We've been told not to masturbate for 24 hours before matches because it'll spoil our performance. Is this true?
Jon, 15 years

No. This is one of many masturbation myths. People once thought that masturbation would weaken your body, and, although totally false, the story lives on. What you do with your body is your own business and nobody else's.

Do older people still masturbate if they're married or living together?
Terri, 15 years

Many people do. They may do it on their own, or with – or to – their partner.

If I don't have sex or anything, will all the sperm build up in my balls and make them burst?
Leroy, 14 years

No: unused sperm are stored for a while until they get old, and then they are reabsorbed into your body and replaced.

I heard that masturbation changes how the vulva looks. Will my doctor be able to tell that I do it?
Thea, 17 years

No. Masturbation does not change your genitals, so nobody can tell. But don't worry if you ever need to tell your doctor that you masturbate (if you have some sexual problem, for instance): they know that it is normal.

RELATIONSHIPS AND EMOTIONS

Your changing feelings   *You and your friends*

Your social life   *Looking at others*

Starting a relationship

Your sexual preference   *Emotional decisions*

Your changing feelings

In adolescence, your feelings may be changing as fast as your body. You may feel things more deeply and be more emotional. You may be happy one day, miserable or irritable the next. This is a tumultuous time – it may even be an exciting one.

When I look at myself in the mirror, I hate myself. I'm too fat and my hair is all wrong. When I go out I feel like everyone is looking at me.

Marisa, 16 years

FEELING SELF-CONSCIOUS

Your body is changing so rapidly that it may seem that everything – hair, shape, and skin – is wrong. You may feel awkward and self-conscious, or worried that you are not attractive. Everyone has their good points physically, whether a smile, freckles, shining eyes, or dimples in their cheeks. And we all know that it isn't just looks that makes people attractive; a sense of humour and friendliness, for example, are just as important.

FRIENDSHIPS

Your relationships with the people around you tend to become more intense. Friends become more important: friendships made in adolescence last longer than those made when you were a child, and when a friendship does break up, as it probably will, it can be especially painful.

You might want to make friends with a particular boy or girl but are too shy to do anything about it. It often feels more comfortable to form friendships as part of a group at first; a one-to-one relationship can then develop naturally.

INDEPENDENCE AND CONFLICT

Your relationship with your parents will probably change dramatically during these years, as you begin to develop your independence. It can still be close, but not quite the same. There may be things that you don't want to talk to them about – not because you are doing anything wrong, but simply because you feel that these are areas that belong exclusively to you. It is common for these feelings of independence to lead to conflict.

You may feel that your parents expect too much of you, or perhaps they want you to be different from the way you are. When you were younger, you probably accepted that the way your parents led their lives was the way you would lead yours. But now you may start to examine the beliefs and attitudes you have been brought up with, and to question whether or not they are really best for you. This can lead to conflict in families. It is not always easy for parents to accept their children's different views and attitudes. Ideally it should be possible for you and your parents to discuss these issues openly and avoid conflict and rows.

UNDERSTANDING YOUR PARENTS' FEELINGS

Sex is often an uncomfortable subject between parents and children. Some parents find it difficult to accept that their child is growing up sexually. No matter what your parents' experience was at your age, they will probably feel differently when it comes to you. You may find that your parents read sex and danger into every situation, or they refuse to accept your sexuality, or that they change the subject whenever sex is mentioned. You might find yourself educating them; there are leaflets available at health and advisory centres that give advice to children and parents.

It's natural for a loving parent to worry, especially when you start to go out on your own. If you can discuss these sorts of concerns, you may be able to agree that you will, say, ring up if you are going to be late.

SEXUAL THOUGHTS AND FEELINGS

Sometimes your sexual feelings may be so strong that they make it hard to think about anything else. These feelings need someone to focus on and this can be almost anyone. It is very common to have a crush on a teacher or an unattainable rock star, even though you know realistically that there is no hope of forming a real relationship. However strong your feelings are, don't let them fool you. They probably don't mean that you are emotionally ready to start a sexual relationship yet.

I know I ought not to worry and nag but unless she's okay, I worry and I can't sleep. Now she rings me if she is coming home late and then I can relax.

Derek, father

QUESTIONS AND ANSWERS

I'm writing to this girl I met on holiday. My parents are always asking me about her. They seem to think they have a right to know everything. Do they?
Mike, 15 years

It sounds as though your parents can't accept that your emotional life is private, perhaps because they are afraid you may be hurt and they want to protect you. However, your feelings are your own and very personal – you do not have to share them with anyone else unless you want to. Let your parents know gently that you want some privacy.

Sometimes I feel like bursting into tears – for no reason at all, really. My mother always says I'm just in one of my moods and tells me to snap out of it. But how am I supposed to do that?
Sarah, 14 years

You can't snap out of it just like that. But you will feel better if you tell someone how you feel: talking to a friend may help you to see things differently. Activity helps these moods too, the more physical the better. Remember that when you are feeling low, everything looks bleak, and that this is just a passing mood.

You and your friends

Childhood friendships don't always last. It's when you start secondary school that you begin to make the friendships that may last for the rest of your life. It is with these friends that you will want to spend time and share your secrets.

My best friend and I always chat for ages every day, and we talk about everything. If anything's wrong, we can always cheer each other up.

Amy, 12 years

BEATING SHYNESS

It's hard to stop being shy, but you can learn to act as if you're not.

Practise playing the part of a non-shy person: it will eventually become natural.

Look at the person you are talking to. If you look past them or down at your feet, you will look bored.

Try to forget about yourself. Concentrate on other people and what's going on around you.

Pretend that the other person is shy, and try to put them at their ease.

If you get tongue-tied, at least ask a question or make a comment, even if "brilliant" is all you say.

BEING A GOOD FRIEND

Being part of a group of friends makes you feel you belong. If your friends like you, you feel good about yourself. This can work both ways: if you feel good about yourself, people will like you. If you are unkind, over-critical, or only ever talk about yourself, you won't be much in demand as a friend.

Your friends will probably come from amongst your classmates at school, or people you share interests with or who live nearby. The most popular people don't necessarily make the best friends. People who seem different from you in some way may pleasantly surprise you if you make the first move.

A good friend is often the person with whom you share all the ups and downs of becoming an adult, exchanging the secrets you wouldn't dream of discussing with your parents. However, once you make friends, you have to give and take. Even the best of friendships can go through difficult times.

RESISTING PRESSURE FROM FRIENDS

Most people want to be like their friends, dress like them, look like them, go where they go, and do what they do. Most of all, they value the opinion of their friends, and being part of a group and all the strengths and security that this offers. Sometimes it can be hard to resist when your friends try to persuade you to do something you don't feel like doing, such as smoking, trying drugs, or playing truant from school. Experimentation is part of growing up, but it's up to you to decide when and if you want to experiment. You may also be under pressure to have sex before you feel ready for it.

Whenever you are under this kind of pressure, the most important thing to remember is that you don't have to lose good friends over it. Friends who drop you if you don't do everything they do are not worth having in the long run: good friends will respect you if you are your own person, and not just a mirror of them. This can take real guts because it isn't comfortable to be left out. You don't have to be critical, you can just say "It doesn't feel right for me". The more sure of yourself you sound, the less pressure there is likely to be.

STARTING TO DATE

Most of your closest friends will probably be of your own sex. You might be interested in the opposite sex, think about them, and talk about them with your friends, but you may not feel quite as comfortable with them as you do with your own sex.

Going around in a mixed group of friends is often the easiest way to get to know each other. Couples may pair off within the group, but you might find yourself dating just to prove that you can, rather than because you really enjoy someone's company. These first relationships may not last very long, but they do help you to experience closer relationships based on sexual attraction. By the time you're 17 or 18, you may be much better able to make more serious relationships.

FEELING LEFT OUT

Making and keeping friends is not always easy. You may feel as if you are the odd one out, that everyone else is having a great time, and that you are the only one who is feeling insecure and shy. But these are very common feelings, shared by even apparently confident people.

If you find it hard to make friends, remember that they don't just fall into your lap. Everyone has to work to make friends, and if you always wait around for others to make the first move, you may have to wait a long time. You could choose the active route – join a youth club, take up a hobby, or play a sport outside school.

There's a boy in our class who has a really rough time because his mother buys him these awful clothes. I feel sorry for him, but if I talk to him, I'll get picked on too.
Kevin, 13 years

FRIENDSHIP
Shared interests provide the basis for friendship – these might include an interest in music, cinema, fashion, books or partying.

Your social life

It is natural as you grow up that you'll want to spend more time with your own friends. Going places and doing things with friends who are interested in the same sorts of things is the start of an exciting new phase in your social life.

All my friends smoke, but I just coughed and felt horrible. It's too expensive anyway.

Clare, 16 years

YOUR CLOSEST FRIENDS
As adolescence progresses, groups of boys and girls mix more, even though your closest friends may still be your own sex.

FREEDOM TO BE YOURSELF

Sometimes you may feel that you are quite a different person with your friends than you are at home. Your parents may have a strong idea of the type of person you are, and so it is not easy to step out of character without them making some comment. You may want to try out a different personality just as you try on different clothes to see whether they suit you. With your friends you can adopt different roles, experiment with different personalities, and see what feels right for you. Sometimes this can cause friction at home because your parents may not approve of the way they see you are changing.

PARENTS AND FRIENDS

If your parents dislike or disapprove of your friends, it is probably because they don't know them. Maybe they have formed an impression based solely on the way your friends look or dress. It may help if you use your home as a base for your social life for a while; when your parents get to know your friends better they may understand why you like them. If they refuse to accept these friendships, and you truly value your friends, you are left with the difficult choice of giving up your friends, or confronting your parents and asking them to trust you.

SMOKING AND DRINKING

Your social life will probably bring you into contact with alcohol, cigarettes, and drugs. Alcohol and drugs help to lower your inhibitions and if you aren't careful they may lead you to behave less cautiously than usual. Many unprotected sexual experiences happen as the result of being temporarily out of control.

Illegal drugs are a problem for some people but virtually everyone has to learn to handle those potentially dangerous drugs that are legal – alcohol and tobacco. Cigarettes can make you feel more relaxed, and more grown up. However, tobacco carries real health risks and it is also very addictive; 85 percent of teenagers who smoke become permanently hooked. On the positive side, if you hold off until you are 20, you are unlikely to start.

Most people manage to learn to drink sensibly and safely without becoming dependent on alcohol. Ideally, home is the best place to learn to do this. With experience you'll learn to judge when you've had enough. There are guidelines issued by government health departments about what constitutes sensible drinking for adults – no more than 21 glasses a week for men and 14 glasses a week for women (a glass is equal to one glass of wine, one measure of spirits or 250 ml (½pt) of beer).

My parents are so concerned about the furniture, I couldn't ask my friends home. Something would get broken. It's better to hang out at the pub or at the park.

Josh, 17 years

QUESTIONS AND ANSWERS

Why is it that I only have two or three drinks and I start feeling drunk very quickly?
Naomi, 16 years

Girls shouldn't try to keep pace with boys. With the same amount of alcohol in the bloodstream, girls become drunk much more quickly because their bodies contain less water than boys. Have a meal or snack before you drink. You get drunk more quickly if your stomach is empty. Have some water or soft drinks first to quench your thirst. Avoid spirits; try to stick to wine and beer. Learn to say no and switch to soft drinks when you've had enough.

What is sensible drinking?
Oliver, 17 years

It is sensible to limit your alcohol intake to two drinks on a couple of days a week. (Everyone should try to have alcohol-free days.) Binge drinking is dangerous because this is when accidents happen, especially if you drink and drive. Don't take lifts from anyone you know has been drinking, and never drive yourself if you have been drinking.

Why is my boyfriend quite aggressive when he drinks?
Anna, 16 years

Alcohol changes behaviour. Often people don't realize how much until friends tell them the next day what they did while they were drunk. Tell your boyfriend that you don't like the side of his character that shows itself when he drinks too much.

It's really hard to avoid drugs at the parties I go to. What should I do about this?
Emily, 16 years

You should never be afraid to say no if you don't want to use drugs. If some of your friends are experimenting with drugs, you may be tempted to experiment yourself. You have to make up your mind if the risks are worth running. If you do experiment, find out all you can about the drug first so that you know what the dangers are. Ecstasy, for example, can cause dangerous dehydration unless plenty of water is drunk with it. Never experiment on your own; make sure you are with people you know and trust.

I got pregnant because I was drunk, and I didn't even ask if he used a condom. I really don't remember much.

Annette, 16 years

Looking at others

Everyone has expectations of themselves and of others, and these may not always be realistic or fair. Sometimes they are based on stereotypes that can affect the way we see the world. Real people, however, don't conform to such patterns.

WHAT IS A STEREOTYPE?

Stereotypes are generalizations about groups of people – perhaps a social class or from other countries – and they are often the root cause of prejudice. Stereotypes are inaccurate and unfair. They encourage you to think of someone as a type because of their gender or colour or appearance, for example, rather than as an individual.

REJECTING SOME OLD IDEAS

In the last 30 years social attitudes have changed in many ways. These changes have made it easier for both men and women to break out of many of their traditional roles if they want to – girls play football, women work outside the home, boys experiment with clothes, and take on more domestic roles.

Old rules about sexual relationships need not apply today. There's no good reason, for example, why a girl shouldn't ask

> *The first thing dad said when I told him I was gay was "You can't be. You were always on the football team." He just couldn't believe it.*
>
> Mark, 18 years

HAPPY FAMILIES

More marriages used to last, partly because they were expected to, and partly because divorce was difficult. Today in the United Kingdom one in three marriages now end in divorce. In the United States, the number is two out of every three, and in Australia and New Zealand one out of every three marriages fails.

QUESTIONS AND ANSWERS

My parents have told me that they are separating and probably getting a divorce. What can I do?
Katrina, 14 years

If your parents are divorcing, try to understand that they are trying to be more honest by parting than staying together. If the atmosphere at home has been very bad, it may even be a relief to you that they have decided to divorce. But if they are so preoccupied with their problems that they are unaware of your anxieties, talk to your brothers and sisters or a close friend. You can give real comfort to each other in this situation. If you are really distressed and have no one to turn to, there are telephone helplines with counsellors who can give you advice
(*see pages 92-93*).

My friend picks on me about not having a dad. I want to tell him to shut up. What should I say?
David, 15 years

The two-parent, married, heterosexual couple is widely regarded as "normal", although it is far from being the only model. Being a good parent need not have anything to do with being married or single, or with being straight or gay. Conventional married couples don't necessarily make good parents – successful parenting depends on the ability of the people involved to have a loving and caring relationship with their children. Tell your friend you feel happy with your parent, and that he should look at people not as stereotypes but as individuals. Perhaps he isn't such a good friend!

a boy out. The best relationships are based on honesty and equality and have no set roles. Sometimes one of you will want to be cuddled and cared for, sometimes the other; sometimes one person will have definite ideas about where to go or what to do. You don't have to fit in with someone else's idea of how you ought to behave.

TREATING GIRLS DIFFERENTLY

There is one persistent stereotype that most of us recognize, and that won't go away. A boy who boasts about his sexual exploits and has many different sexual partners is regarded as a real man, and one of the lads. On the other hand, a girl who sleeps with a number of different boys is sometimes branded as loose and easy. The message is that girls shouldn't have any sexual desires, or at any rate they shouldn't do anything about them. This is patently unequal treatment and untrue. Most people are a mixture of characteristics, and it is better to view people as individuals than to prejudge them on the basis of sex, race, or class.

I'm much better at maths and science than most of the boys in our class, but I feel I have to keep quiet.

Sue, 14 years

ENRICHING EXPERIENCE
If you live in a multi-cultural area, you will probably mix with people whose backgrounds are very different from your own.

Starting a relationship

You know instinctively that you want to get to know someone better, but probably not why. If you do make the first move, maybe you'll be turned down, or maybe in a few weeks time you'll be wondering why you hesitated even for a minute.

THE PERFECT PARTNER

Most people think they have some idea of their ideal type. Quite often, however, you find yourself falling for someone totally different whom you may not even have been particularly attracted to at first sight. Friendship, good conversation, a sense of humour, liking the same music and fashions are the sorts of things that might attract you to a particular person.

SHOWING AND SAYING HOW YOU FEEL

You can show that you like someone by seeking out their company, looking into their eyes a bit more than usual when you talk, or touching them casually – a hand on their arm to attract their attention, for example. If someone shows this kind of interest in you, it's up to you how you respond. If you feel the same, you can smile back, hold their gaze, and not move away. If you want to put them off, you can be a bit aloof without being rude, giving them a cue to back off.

Body language works, up to a point, but it is more honest to say what you feel. Once you are over the "getting-to-know-you" stage, it will save you a lot of misunderstandings if you can tell each other, as well as show each other, how you

I knew he liked me, but he just wouldn't say anything. So I went and sat beside him at lunch and got talking, and after that everything was fine.

Jenny, 15 years

ATTRACTION

It's no accident that lovers tend to gaze into one another's eyes. The pupil in the eye widens when we look at something that interests or attracts us. Most of us agree on what makes a "beautiful" face, but differ on what we find sexually attractive. Statistically, physical appearance matters more to men, while women are usually attracted by a man's intelligence and sense of humour rather than looks.

Pupils narrow

Pupils widen

feel. Of course, you probably won't like everyone who likes you, so you may have to tell someone you're not interested. If someone you aren't really interested in approaches you, remember that they have had to pluck up the courage to ask you out, so it is kinder to be polite if you're not interested rather than cruelly reject someone.

COMING ON STRONG

Trying to get too close to someone too soon is usually a big mistake. You can't force someone to like you. Look for cues that you are moving too fast, and slow down. If you draw attention to yourself, tell too many jokes, or praise people profusely because you want them to like you, you can start to look desperate.

At the start of a relationship, it is often hard not to try to take over the other person completely. But relationships need time to grow. Resist the temptation to demand that your boy or girlfriend be with you all the time.

THREE'S A CROWD

It can happen to anyone: you like someone a friend of yours is going out with. What should you do? You could show that you're interested, but the chances are that you will lose your friend this way. You could also ask your friend how serious the relationship is. You have to decide which means most to you – your friendship or a possible future relationship. It can be just as difficult to find that you are interested in a friend of the person you're going out with. Think carefully before you give any kind of come-on. Of the three of you, at least one will get hurt, and it could be you.

GOOD RELATIONSHIPS

Falling in love can be wonderful. Your heart pounds and there are butterflies in your stomach, and you'll long to be together every moment and think about each other compulsively. A good relationship is one that increases your self-esteem and your personal happiness. It is also one that is based on respect for each other, good communication, and trust. Being good friends is vital in a relationship.

You may find yourself enjoying going out and socializing more; or you may just be happy being alone together. You may find yourself listening to someone else's views more intently. It is not always easy to tell the short-term infatuation from the relationship that lasts. You are bound to make a few mistakes as you are growing up. You'll probably look back later and wonder what you ever saw in the person who was the most important person in your life when you were younger.

I didn't ask this girl out for ages – I was afraid she'd turn me down or laugh. She said yes, though, and she said she'd been waiting for me to say something. I had no idea!

Keith, 15 years

I went out with this girl for a few weeks, thinking this is it! Then suddenly I realized I didn't want to see her any more – she looks fantastic, but she's a bit boring when you get to know her.

Sean, 16 years

Your sexual preference

Part of growing up is discovering what your main sexual preferences are. This can be difficult if you feel unsure, and you may worry that you are different if you find yourself attracted to your own sex (homosexuality) or to both sexes (bisexuality).

EXPRESSING YOUR SEXUALITY

Few people go through life without ever having felt attracted to someone of their own sex. Teenagers often have passionate sexual feelings for a friend or a teacher. Studies show that a significant proportion of men have had some sexual experience with other men. Girls are just as likely to have homosexual feelings. For many, this is a practice stage of sexual development, but others continue to be attracted by their own sex at some times in their lives, and by the opposite sex at others. However, it is usual for a steady preference for one sex or the other to emerge, although there are people who remain bisexual.

WHAT CAUSES THESE FEELINGS?

Nobody knows exactly why some people are attracted to their own sex and others to the opposite sex. Some people feel from an early age that they have always known that they are gay or lesbian. For others, this realization can happen at any time in their lives. It may not be until you are in your twenties that you feel certain that your feelings about your sexuality are not going to change. If you don't know anyone who is gay or lesbian, you may feel very much on your own.

COMING TO TERMS WITH HOMOSEXUALITY

Because society treats heterosexuality as the norm, young people who are homosexual often feel particularly isolated. If you think you are gay or lesbian, remember that there are lots of support groups and advice lines you can contact in person or by telephone (*see pages 92-93*). You will feel less isolated once you have met other gays and lesbians.

However, there is no denying that there is prejudice against homosexuals. If you feel that you are attracted to your own sex, you may be tempted to keep quiet about it when you hear your schoolmates use "gay" as a term of

> **I think my parents hoped they could cure me of being gay and that it was all just in my imagination.**
>
> Mark, 18 years

FINDING OUT
Once you've accepted your own feelings, you'll discover that there are plenty of other people who feel like you do.

abuse. Being gay or lesbian is part of what you are, like your hair colour or the size of your nose. The problems are created by other people's prejudice and intolerance. Knowing this, some gay and lesbian people choose to try to ignore their feelings or disguise their sexuality. This can cause a great deal of unhappiness. If you are sure of your feelings, you may feel more comfortable if you can at least tell the truth to those who matter most to you.

TELLING YOUR PARENTS

One hard decision to make for anyone who knows they are gay or lesbian is whether to tell their parents. Your parents may be upset at first and will almost certainly need time to get used to the idea. Most people think that there is only one way to live and be happy and that is their way. They may think that unless you have a conventional marriage with children, you won't be happy. And whatever their own feelings, they know also that gays and lesbians are often treated unfairly. They'll be afraid for you.

However, the advantages of telling your parents and not having to keep a very important part of your life secret are enormous. It is quite possible that your parents may have guessed anyway. Loving parents can eventually accept that their child is gay or lesbian.

You may feel that you need a trial run before you tell your parents. A close family friend might be a good person to tell first. They can act as your support when you eventually broach the subject with your parents. A close friend whom you can trust and who will listen and be sympathetic is also a vital source of support. If there isn't anyone you feel you can trust, contact a counselling organizations (*see page 92-93*). By joining a contact group you'll feel more comfortable and confident with your feelings.

BEING TOGETHER
A loving relationship with someone they care about is what most people want, whether thay are gay, lesbian or straight.

> ❝ *When I called the helpline I realized that she was the first lesbian person I had knowingly talked to. It felt really liberating.* ❞
>
> Sue, 16 years

QUESTIONS AND ANSWERS

What is it that gay and lesbian people do?
Jane, 16 years

Gays and lesbians lead normal lives in which they experience the same sexual and emotional feelings as heterosexuals. They want to be near one another, kiss, and make love like heterosexual people. They can show their sexual feelings by masturbating one another, oral sex or anal sex.

Is it true that gay men molest small boys?
Edward, 14 years

Gay men are no more likely to be interested in small boys than heterosexual men are in small girls. Normal adults prefer their sexual partners to be adults. You should be very wary of any adult who seems interested in you in an overtly sexual way and talk to someone you trust about it.

THE LAW

Lesbianism is not illegal because it doesn't exist in law. Homosexual intercourse is illegal in the United Kingdom under the age of 18. In Australia and New Zealand homosexual intercourse is generally illegal under 18. As the age of consent for heterosexual acts is usually around 16, this represents an institutionalized prejudice against gays (*see page 44*).

Emotional decisions

Being in love is wonderful. You feel so many confused emotions and exciting sensations, like tingles up your spine when you hear a person's voice on the phone. It does take time to learn how to handle these feelings and emotions.

We really love each other, but I feel I've met the right person at the wrong time. I wish I could just put the whole thing on ice for five years.

Amy, 16 years

MAKING IT WORK

In the first flush of love, you may think your partner is perfect, but after this infatuation passes, you begin to see each other as real people. If there's nothing much between you but sexual attraction, you may become a bit bored and irritated in a very short time. Infatuation and a lasting relationship are not the same thing.

Learning how to handle a relationship takes work, and this is one reason why your first relationships might be brief. This can be shattering and rejection can be painful. But you do learn more with each relationship. What you get from a relationship is, more or less, what you put into it.

THINKING OF OTHERS

When you are in a relationship, you'll find yourself thinking about your partner a lot of the time. If things change a little, don't take this too personally. Your partner may have moods that have got nothing to do with you, so ask them what's wrong, rather than be offended and sulky. Learning to communicate in a relationship is very important. This means being able to express what you want as well as finding out about your partner's needs.

BEING OUT OF STEP

Boys and girls tend to be out of step with each other in their teens. Emotionally, girls usually grow up more quickly than boys; a boy of 15 can seem very childish to a girl of the same age. As a result, some girls are likely to be interested in more mature boys. Because of this, girls often come under pressure to have sex earlier than they might want to, especially if they go out with older boys or men.

HOW FAR SHOULD YOU GO?

Films, magazines, and books all seem to assume that there's only one road for a relationship to go down, and it ends in bed. This is nonsense. You are the one who decides how far along the road you want to go, and you can stop at any time.

HOW TO SAY NO

Saying no when you are confronted with a difficult social or sexual situation takes practice.

■ Body language gives the other person the hint quite quickly. Straighten up and move back, keeping some distance between you so that you can get your thoughts clear.

■ Practise saying no in situations where it is justified – if your little brother or sister is being unreasonably demanding, or if someone wants to borrow a pen that you need too.

■ Don't give in to bullying by being made to feel different. Recognize that threats can be hidden. For example, someone might say: "If you don't have sex, you'll be the only virgin in your group."

You may not want a sexual relationship yet, or not with this person. You may have strong religious, cultural, and personal views about sex outside marriage and you should not be afraid to uphold these views.

You'll meet plenty of people whom you like, even love, but want nothing more than a kiss or a hug from, and who may feel the same about you. It is possible to have a loving and caring relationship without sex. The most important thing is to make clear what *you* want, and to make your own choices after thinking them through, especially if you think that the other person might have something else in mind. If you don't know what you want, say so. You need to be assertive about something as important as a sexual relationship. You have a right to make up your own mind without being pressured and no one should force you into having full penetrative sex that you don't want or don't feel ready for.

THE RIGHT TIME AND THE RIGHT PERSON

When you have reached the age of consent – and this differs from state to state and country to country – you can have sexual intercourse legally. This doesn't mean it's compulsory and it is usually too early for most people. While a 16-year-old, for example, is physically old enough to have sexual intercourse and to have a baby, few 16-year-olds are emotionally mature enough to deal with the commitments and responsibilities involved in a lasting sexual relationship.

There are no prizes for starting early; this is one of the hardest areas to be truthful about when your friends start and you don't want to be left out. You shouldn't always believe what you hear – statistics show that by the age of 17 just under half of all boys and about a third of girls will have had sexual intercourse – so someone isn't telling the truth! If you have doubts, or feel you have to ask for more advice and guidance (*see pages 92-93*), then you are probably not ready to have sex just yet. There are so many pressures to experience sex that it is difficult to reach your own decision.

If you are determined to have sex, make sure it is planned and protected (*see page 54*). Statistics show that early sexual

WHEN TO SAY NO

If you are thinking of having sex for any of the following reasons, it is better to say no.

■ To prove you love someone or as proof of their love.

■ To prove you can (everyone can!).

■ To satisfy your curiosity.

■ Because you're afraid that you will lose your boy or girl friend if you don't.

■ Because you've been talked into it.

■ Because you are drunk or high on drugs.

■ Because you're in a position where the other person expects it.

Mum started telling me to go on the pill when she saw I was getting serious with Tony. I know she meant well, but I can make up my own mind about when I want to sleep with someone.
Jill, 17 years

BREAKING UP

Breaking up can be much worse if you don't know why it happens. If the person you want to be with won't answer the phone or letters, you may know that it is over, but if they don't talk to you, you might just keep hoping. It is always kinder to tell someone when a relationship is over.

I thought I'd never get over it. Then my friend persuaded me to go out with her and I met Alan. I thought, here we go, I never thought I'd feel like this again.
Melanie, 16 years

experiences are often unplanned and unprotected. Your first sexual experience can be fantastic or a tremendous let-down – even if it is the right person, the right time, and the right place. This first experience is seen as a rite of passage, and an important point in your life – a pity to waste it with the wrong person and at the wrong time.

WHEN FEELINGS CHANGE

Relationships don't stand still. One person might want to get more serious, while the other still wants to see other people. You have to decide whether you want to go on with a relationship like this, or if it is too painful.

It hurts to discover that the other person doesn't feel as deeply as you do, and it can be just as hard to find that you don't love someone as much as you hoped you might. It takes courage to end things when you still care for the other person, but it might be necessary. Having sex within this relationship won't save it either, nor will it stop your partner from moving on.

LETTING SOMEONE DOWN GENTLY

It's always painful for both people involved when a relationship breaks up. You may not believe that you'll ever be happy again, but you will – even if it takes weeks, or months, for it to happen. It helps to talk, so seek out a friend you can trust. It probably isn't sensible to keep hoping; you will make yourself more miserable. A definite goodbye may hurt, but everything will be easier once you have accepted that the relationship is over. You can go forward, wounded a little but stronger and wiser for the experience.

THE AGE OF CONSENT

The age of consent in the United Kingdom is 16 years (17 in Ireland). In New Zealand and in most states of Australia it is 16 for females but 21 for males in Western Australia, and 18 in the Northern Territory. It is 17 for both sexes in South Australia and Tasmania. The age of consent for homosexual acts is different (*see page 41*).

QUESTIONS AND ANSWERS

My friends all keep warning me off this girl I like at school, because she treated her last boyfriend really badly. But can't things be different for us?
Martin, 16 years

Seeing how people have behaved in other relationships is a clue to their behaviour but not necessarily an obvious one. It may have been that boys have treated your girlfriend badly in the past because she hasn't been careful enough about which boys she went out with and her reputation has been tainted through no fault of her own. Hurt pride can cause people to be spiteful.

My boyfriend and I have been together for six months and we get on really well together, but we don't have a lot in common. Do you think this matters?
Kirsten, 16 years

You don't have to call the whole thing off because you don't share a passion for the same things. Similar personalities, backgrounds, or interests are all pluses in any relationship, but although they help, they aren't essential. As long as you enjoy each other's company, there isn't a problem; it is probably the differences that attract you to each other.

WHAT HAPPENS DURING SEX

Sexual intercourse

The first time

Enjoying sex

Dealing with difficulties

Sexual intercourse

Sexual intercourse, or making love, is an intimate form of contact between two people. Its biological function is to enable a woman to become pregnant, but when couples have sex they mostly do so simply because they enjoy it.

FOREPLAY AND AROUSAL

A couple arouse each other by holding, caressing, and kissing: this is called foreplay. They can stroke or kiss the sensitive areas of each other's bodies – the stomach, inner thighs, buttocks, nipples, and around the highly sensitive genitals. The smell and taste of a partner's skin and genitals enhance sexual excitement.

During foreplay, the body's senses are stimulated, sending messages to the brain, which, in turn, sends messages to the genitals and other parts of the body, preparing them for sex and increasing excitement. Many men and some women can be sexually aroused by the sight of their partner's body and the thought of sex.

WHAT HAPPENS WHEN SOMEONE IS AROUSED

When people are aroused, their heart and breathing rates increase, and their bodies feel super-sensitive. Both sexes also experience changes in their genitals. Arousal increases blood flow into the penis, causing it to extend, darken, and become erect. As the man becomes more excited, his penis reaches its maximum length and thickness. When a woman is aroused,

We spend more time on foreplay before sex than we used to, and we both have better orgasms – they're more intense.

Nick, 18 years

I get really hot during sex, and my heart just pounds. It's better exercise than working out!

Leonie, 17 years

QUESTIONS AND ANSWERS

How often should you have sex? Is having it every day too much?
Zoë, 16 years

There are no rules: couples should do what feels right and comfortable.

How long should you spend on foreplay before having sex?
Barry, 17 years

Foreplay should be long enough for both partners to become excited enough to enjoy intercourse. Men sometimes forget that women can take longer to become aroused than men. Surveys show that many

women, and some men, feel that foreplay is too short, often lasting five or ten minutes, and should last much longer – 30 minutes or more.

A friend told me sex isn't proper without intercourse. But can't you have orgasms in other ways?
Darryl, 16 years

Sex needn't mean intercourse. Some couples regularly have sex without intercourse *(see page 48)*, arousing each other in other ways, and the orgasms they have are just as satisfying. Some couples look on this as practising safer sex.

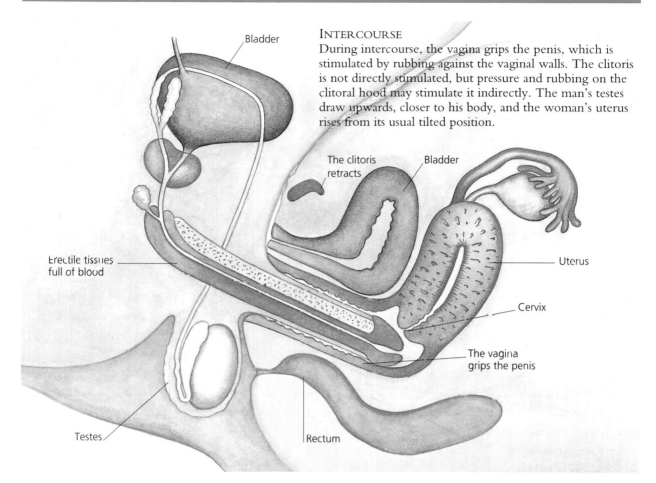

Bladder

INTERCOURSE
During intercourse, the vagina grips the penis, which is stimulated by rubbing against the vaginal walls. The clitoris is not directly stimulated, but pressure and rubbing on the clitoral hood may stimulate it indirectly. The man's testes draw upwards, closer to his body, and the woman's uterus rises from its usual tilted position.

The clitoris retracts

Bladder

Erectile tissues full of blood

Uterus

Cervix

The vagina grips the penis

Testes

Rectum

the blood flow to her vulva and vagina increases. Her vagina becomes coated with lubricating mucus, and the inner part of it expands, while the outer part narrows. Her clitoris becomes erect, emerging from its hood of skin, and her nipples become erect and more sensitive. As she grows more excited, her clitoris retracts, and her vaginal lips become bigger and darker.

INTERCOURSE AND ORGASM
When both partners are aroused, they may both feel ready for penetration (when the man's penis enters the vagina), though there are other ways of reaching orgasm (*see page 51*) without penetration. Orgasm is experienced by both sexes as a series of deep and pleasurable waves that spread throughout the whole body. Men and women don't necessarily reach orgasm in the same way and at the same time. The man often experiences orgasm as he ejaculates. A woman may not have an orgasm unless the clitoris is directly stimulated. Girls don't always find early experiences of sex orgasmic for this reason. Gradually men and women learn what gives them pleasure so they can let their partner know what they want. After ejaculation, the penis becomes limp and the man's excitement disappears. The woman's body returns to normal more gradually.

When my boyfriend comes, he sort of stops breathing for a few seconds and then makes this strangled sound and starts gasping like he's just run the marathon. I thought there was something seriously wrong with him at first.

Julia, 18 years

The first time

Most people never forget the first time they had sex, whether it was better than they expected, a disaster, or somewhere in-between. It's impossible to get everything perfect first time, but it helps if both partners are prepared and understand each other's needs.

When we had sex the first time, I didn't enjoy the actual sex that much. What I did like was cuddling up to my boyfriend all night.

Josie, 17 years

WHEN IS IT SAFE?

If you are not using any contraception, you can get pregnant even if:
■ It is your first time.
■ You made love standing up.
■ Your monthly period has just finished.
■ You wash out your vagina afterwards.
■ Your partner withdraws before ejaculation.
■ You haven't had your first period.
■ Your partner puts a condom on just before penetration (there may be some leakage of sperm beforehand).

THINKING AHEAD

The thought of having sex for the first time can be both exciting and frightening. Both of these emotions can make it difficult to relax, and can cause problems.

It is very important for anyone about to have sex to discuss contraception before they get carried away. Both girls and boys may worry about pregnancy, yet, alarmingly, statistics show that many couples don't use contraception or protection against infection the first time. However, there is *always* a risk of pregnancy and infection. Contraceptives are usually available free from a clinic or doctor *(see page 54)*, and male condoms can be bought over the counter at a pharmacy or supermarket.

Having to rush and worrying about privacy are common reasons for nervousness. For the first time, it helps to be somewhere comfortable rather than in the back of a car.

EXPECTATIONS AND REALITY

Most people want to "get it right", but what they think is right is likely to be based on films or books, and is probably not realistic. Whatever the two of you want to do is right – each couple is unique. One or both of you might have experience already: you may have kissed and caressed, dressed or naked, and have had orgasms from masturbation or oral sex *(see page 51)*. Or it may be the first time you have seen each other naked or touched anyone sexually.

THE IMPORTANCE OF AROUSAL

Men can be aroused just by thinking of sex or seeing their partner's body. A man may be so excited that he ejaculates before intercourse. If a man is nervous, he may find it difficult to have an erection at all. Just kissing and caressing together should solve the problem.

Women generally take longer to become aroused to the point where the vagina opens up and produces lubricating fluid. The vagina may be closed or dry if a woman is nervous or not aroused. If the man is patient and asks what she likes, and if she can show or tell him, these problems can be avoided. If sex is painful, this is possibly because the vagina is not sufficiently lubricated, If extra lubrication is needed, this should be in the form of a special water-based gel such as KY jelly (available from a pharmacy). Petroleum-based lubricants will destroy a male condom. Once a couple feel more confident, lubricant will not be needed.

WILL IT HURT?

Some girls feel pain the first time because their hymen is intact *(see page 15)*, and hurts when it is broken by intercourse. There may even be slight bleeding. It was once believed that a broken hymen meant a girl was not a virgin, but often the opening is either quite large or has been stretched in strenuous sports or by using tampons. Others feel pain because they find it hard to relax the vaginal muscles – they need time to relax and feel comfortable.

HOW WILL IT FEEL?

The first time a couple has sex is often not spectacular; it takes time to get to know each other's bodies and to feel comfortable together. It should improve, but only if there is good communication and attention to each other's needs.

Men may thrust too deeply in the vagina and should try to make sure that they are not hurting their partner. Most men will have an orgasm the first time they have vaginal sex, but most women will not. Like all things that need practice, sex usually gets better after the first time.

I decided to wait until I was 18 before I had sex for the first time; I didn't feel ready before then.

Peter, 18 years

When I tried putting the condom on I just came right away. But we tried again later, and it was fine: I think I was calmer.

Paul, 16 years

QUESTIONS AND ANSWERS

When you see sex in films, women always have orgasms, even the first time. When I had sex the first time, I was expecting fireworks, but nothing happened. Why not?
Terri, 16 years

Films are just unrealistic: most girls don't have an orgasm the first time that they have sex. It may take you time to learn how to respond to your boyfriend, and take him time to learn how to stimulate you to reach orgasm. Many girls and women do not have orgasms during intercourse at all unless they are very aroused, usually by having their clitoris stimulated at the same time. Sex improves with patience and practice.

I've just had sex with my girlfriend for the first time. I really wanted to look at her, but she said she felt too embarrassed. I don't get it – what's wrong with her?
Damon, 17 years

There is nothing wrong with her at all. Seeing your partner naked is very arousing for you, but some people are not used to being seen naked and feel embarrassed. She may be thinking of all the things she believes are wrong with her body. As time goes on, she will probably feel more relaxed and comfortable, and will start to enjoy you looking at, and being aroused by, her body – and looking at you.

Enjoying sex

Sexual enjoyment is all about giving and receiving pleasure, which means it is about communication. People reach orgasm in different ways, and to enjoy sex to the full, couples must tell each other what they like and – just as importantly – what they don't like.

We both decided to try out some different positions. Once I fell off the bed, but otherwise it's been good experience.

Charlie, 17 years

REACHING ORGASM

Sometimes, a couple reach orgasm at the same time; more often, they don't. It doesn't really matter – whoever comes first can continue to stimulate the other to orgasm. Although orgasms are important to most people, they are not the only sexual sensation – there are plenty of others to enjoy.

VARIETY AND EXPERIMENTATION

Experimenting can be fun, provided that both partners are willing participants. Intercourse is not the only way of enjoying sex – foreplay, for example, can be continued until orgasm. This can be a choice for those who would rather postpone full penetrative sex. It can be as enjoyable as intercourse, and it is safer, too, carrying little or no risk of pregnancy (*see page 70*) or of passing on infections (*see pages 80-83*).

TRYING DIFFERENT POSITIONS

Some couples always use the same position for sex; others vary their lovemaking. The many possible positions for intercourse can be divided into two groups: face to face and from behind.

ANAL SEX

This is intercourse with the penis in the anus. Anal sex carries a high risk of infection including HIV if the sexual partner is infected (*see pages 84-85*), and a risk of other infections for women because the anus is full of bacteria that can be spread to the vagina by anal sex.

QUESTIONS AND ANSWERS

I have orgasms from masturbating or from oral sex, but never from intercourse. Will I ever be able to?
Tanya, 17 years

Many men – and women – think that if a man just thrusts away inside a woman long enough she will reach orgasm, but women rarely have orgasms during intercourse unless their clitoris is also stimulated. You could spend more time on foreplay, so that you are more aroused, or one of you could rub your clitoris during intercourse. But don't see orgasm as some goal to be reached: try to enjoy other things about sex.

My boyfriend wants to tie me up when we have sex. I don't really want him to. What should I do? Am I being too boring?
Alex, 17 years

Sex is about doing what you *want* to do, and you should never be forced into doing anything that you don't want to. What your boyfriend wants to do is bondage, which some people – but not all – enjoy. He probably wants to see you, and have sex with you, while you are in a submissive position. If you don't feel comfortable with this, you don't have to do it: tell him firmly that you will not.

In face-to-face positions, a couple can see, touch, and arouse each other. The most used position is with the man or woman on top; this is not necessarily the most satisfactory position for the woman because there is little clitoral stimulation. Other positions include side-by-side, seated, and standing. The chosen position is likely to be one that is comfortable for the individuals.

If the man enters the woman from behind, he can easily stimulate her breasts and clitoris. The most used position is often called the "doggie" position: the woman kneels on her hands and knees, and the man kneels behind her. Other positions include standing and side-by-side.

ORAL SEX

Oral sex means stimulating a partner's genitals with the lips and tongue. Couples may use oral sex as part of foreplay, or may carry on to orgasm as an alternative to intercourse. Licking or kissing a woman's clitoris is called cunnilingus, while kissing and sucking a man's penis is known as fellatio. By being in control when stimulating the man, the woman can determine whether the man ejaculates in her mouth. Like all sexual contact, oral sex is more pleasant if the genitals are clean. Oral sex avoids the risks of pregnancy, but a genital infection or cold sores near the mouth can be transmitted during oral sex; there is also a small risk of contracting HIV (*see page 84*).

> *Although I'm on the pill, I still get my boyfriend to wear a condom as well – for safer sex.*
>
> Cheryl, 17 years

POSITIONS FOR SEX

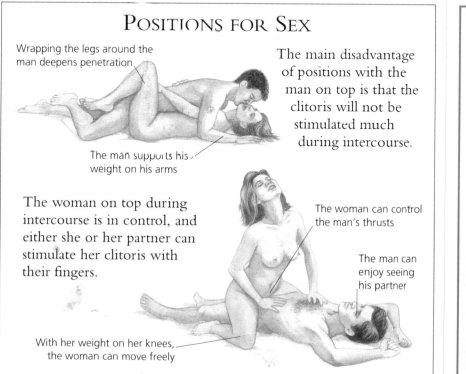

Wrapping the legs around the man deepens penetration

The man supports his weight on his arms

The main disadvantage of positions with the man on top is that the clitoris will not be stimulated much during intercourse.

The woman on top during intercourse is in control, and either she or her partner can stimulate her clitoris with their fingers.

The woman can control the man's thrusts

The man can enjoy seeing his partner

With her weight on her knees, the woman can move freely

GUIDELINES FOR EXPERIMENTATION

If you want to experiment with your sex life, you must be able to trust each other and you must be very clear about what you want.

■ Never be pushed into doing anything that you really don't want to do.
■ Never try to persuade an unwilling partner into doing anything: it isn't fair.
■ Agree in advance exactly what you want to do.
■ If your partner wants you to stop at any point, do so. You must respect their feelings and wishes.
■ Don't do anything that could be harmful or might hurt either of you.
■ Don't do anything that makes you feel ashamed – it isn't right for you.

Dealing with difficulties

It is not unusual to have sexual difficulties, whatever your age or experience. Sex is a sharing experience, not a test of your abilities, and a couple who have a good relationship can overcome most problems by talking them over.

WHY PEOPLE HAVE PROBLEMS

Any problems you might have will probably be caused by poor communication or inexperience, and most vanish with experience and better communication. Perhaps you are not yet ready for a sexual relationship. Some difficulties are the result of anxiety – especially about being a "good performer" – and disappear once you relax. Other problems result from guilt feelings or past experiences. If you think this is likely, it might be best to see a counsellor: a doctor can refer you to one.

PREMATURE EJACULATION AND ERECTION PROBLEMS

Premature ejaculation means coming too early, even before the penis is in the vagina. If the problem persists, the man can learn control by masturbating, stopping just before orgasm.

Failure to get, or maintain, an erection happens to most men at some time, usually because they are tired or anxious, or because they have drunk too much alcohol. Extra stimulation can help, but it may be better to try again later. Worrying about erection problems only makes them worse. If the problems do persist, talk to a doctor in case there is a medical reason.

NOT HAVING AN ORGASM

This is only a problem if it happens persistently. Not all women have orgasms every time they have sex. It takes time for them and their partners to learn how their bodies respond. Tension and anxiety can cause problems, too. Young men seldom have orgasm problems, although some older men do.

PAINFUL INTERCOURSE

If sex is painful for a woman, she may need more time and stimulation. Very rarely women may suffer from vaginismus, where the vaginal muscles tighten, making intercourse impossible. The woman should see her doctor if this persists. In men, a tight foreskin may make erection and intercourse painful. This is rare, and is cured by circumcision *(see page 24)*. In both sexes, infections *(see pages 80-83)* can irritate the genitals so that intercourse is painful.

We'd had a great night and we were in bed but there was nothing happening – I'd had too much to drink. I was so embarrassed – she said I'd better cut down on beer in future, or else!

Greg, 18 years

PREMATURE EJACULATION

This means coming before you want to and it is very common. It is often a shock and a disappointment to a man and his partner. It may happen the first time, or the first few times you have sex, simply because you are experiencing the reality of sexual contact with another person. As you become used to being sexually excited by the sight and touch of your partner, you will gradually develop control of your ejaculation so that you can come when you want to. If you continue to come too quickly, don't feel a failure. If your partner is sympathetic, talk to her. Together, try different ways to make love which don't necessarily focus on you coming in her vagina.

CONTRACEPTION

Choosing contraceptives

Contraceptives are used to prevent unplanned pregnancy. They are easy to get, free in many cases, and advice is confidential. From a first sexual experience, both a man and a woman need to take responsibility for contraception.

RISK OF PREGNANCY

About half of all couples don't use contraceptives the first time they have sex. Some continue not using them, perhaps because they don't know where to get advice or feel too embarrassed to ask. They may think that contraception is the other person's responsibility. Many probably believe that they can get away with it, and some may want a child (*see page 70*). If you have intercourse without contraception, you are always taking a risk. If you don't use contraception, the probability of pregnancy is high, because fertility is highest in early adulthood.

WHERE TO GET CONTRACEPTIVES

Everyone is entitled to free, confidential advice on contraception from doctors (*see right*), or family planning clinics. Condoms can be bought from vending machines or supermarkets as well as pharmacies and clinics. It may seem that it is premeditated and unspontaneous behaviour to organize contraception before becoming sexually active, and many parents may even feel that this will lead to experimentation – but it doesn't need to be viewed this way. It can be seen as being responsible and taking control of your life.

If you think and plan in advance, you can discuss what type of contraceptive you are going to use, and who is going to organize getting it. Whether or not you decide on a method that needs a prescription, both of you could go to a doctor or clinic. Doctors can prescribe most contraceptives, although in some countries they may not. If you really don't want to go to a doctor or clinic, you can always buy condoms.

If you are under 16, the doctor will ask, or may try to persuade, you to

TAKING A LEAD
There is nothing to stop anyone from consulting a doctor or clinic about family planning: condoms are usually free from family planning clinics and doctors. It is completely unfair for boys to leave the contraceptive arrangements up to girls because they are the ones who get pregnant. Boys as well as girls should ask themselves, "Am I ready to become a parent?"

tell your parents that you are using contraceptives, but he or she should respect your wishes if you do not want your parents to be told. Tell your parents if at all possible – they may already suspect that you are thinking about having sex, and be glad to know that you are acting responsibly.

WHAT TO ASK FOR

The contraceptives that are supplied only by a doctor or clinic include the pill, cervical cap, diaphragm, intrauterine device, injectables, and implants. A doctor or clinic can also give advice about natural family planning. You don't have to go to your own doctor; you can choose to go to another doctor for contraception if you wish. Family planning clinics will offer advice on the best method for you – some methods may not be suitable for you because of your family medical history or smoking, for example. If you are at all worried about the advice you are given, ask questions. The important thing is to find the right method for you.

If you are prescribed the pill, your blood pressure and weight will be checked, and if you smoke you might be advised to give up. If you are already sexually active, you may be offered a smear test (*see page 78*) either at the first or at a later visit. Whatever method you choose, you will be seen soon afterwards to check that there are no side effects. Thereafter check–ups are usually every six months.

THE LAW AND CONTRACEPTION

There is no need to be apprehensive about going to your doctor or family planning clinic for advice on contraception. All young people are given confidential advice (free in the UK) on contraception by their doctor, whatever their age. Parental consent is not necessary, although if you are very young, your doctor is legally required to discuss the value of parental support with you, while respecting your wishes for confidentiality.

QUESTIONS AND ANSWERS

I'm a virgin, but I want to start having sex. Can I use a diaphragm?
Janine, 16 years

If you use tampons, you may be able to use a diaphragm. It needs practice, and if you feel nervous about sex at first, you may not want to have to worry about putting the diaphragm in properly. You will be given a practice cap until you are confident.

Can you go on using the diaphragm when you have your period?
Paulette, 17 years

Yes. In fact, the diaphragm will contain bleeding temporarily while a couple make love. It must be left in place as usual after intercourse for at least six hours because there is a small chance that a girl can get pregnant during her period.

If I squirt spermicide into my vagina just before sex, will that kill the sperm?
Marsha, 16 years

No. Spermicides are sperm-killing chemicals but they are not effective enough on their own. They are used with barrier methods (*see pages 63-65*) as an extra precaution.

Why should there be female condoms if there are already male condoms? Is this a way to put the responsibility onto the woman?
Penny, 17 years

Taking responsibility for contraception is something that, ideally, everyone should do. This is a fairly new method of contraception and like most methods it takes time to get used to. Female condoms do protect against infection and unplanned pregnancy.

My boyfriend didn't want to use condoms, because he said they spoilt it for him. I said no condom, no sex – the risk would spoil it for me.

Paula, 17 years

Types of contraceptive

Contraception has been used for over 3,000 years to prevent unplanned pregnancy. All forms of contraception work by preventing the fertilization of a woman's egg by a man's sperm. This is achieved in various ways.

Methods of contraception can be divided roughly into five groups. Barrier methods physically prevent sperm from swimming into the uterus and fertilizing the woman's egg (*see pages 60-65*); hormonal methods alter a woman's hormonal cycle to prevent fertilization (*see pages 58-59*); the intrauterine device (IUD) prevents the sperm from reaching the egg or may prevent the egg from embedding itself in the uterus (*see page 66*); natural methods are based on calculating the time when a woman is least fertile and abstaining or using another method to avoid conception when she is most fertile (*see page 67*); and sterilization is a permanent surgical means of preventing conception (*see page 67*). On the following pages, the advantages, disadvantages and reliability of each of the contraceptive methods is given.

Progestogen-only pill

HORMONAL CONTRACEPTIVES
These work by introducing synthetic versions of female hormones into a woman's body. The hormones either stop her from ovulating, or make her cervical mucus thick, preventing sperm from reaching the uterus.
The hormones are taken by mouth, as an implant under the skin, or by injection.

Injectable hormone

Hormonal implants

INJECTIONS AND IMPLANTS
Some hormonal methods of contraception can only be administered by a doctor or a specially trained family planning nurse. These are injectable contraceptives and implants that have to be inserted under the skin. Both types are long-term and require no attention from the user.

Ring at open end

Female condom

Polyurethane sheath

Ring at closed end

MALE AND FEMALE CONDOMS
Condoms stop sperm from reaching the uterus. The male condom, made of thin rubber, is unrolled over the erect penis. The female condom, made of thin polyurethane, is inserted into the vagina. Whichever type is used by the couple must be put on, or inserted, before intercourse. Both types are thrown away after intercourse and can be used only once.

Flexible ring

Lubricated sheath

Male condom

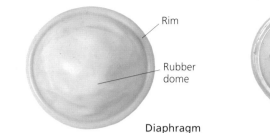

Rim

Rubber
dome

Diaphragm

Rim

Rubber
dome

Cervical cap

DIAPHRAGMS AND CERVICAL CAPS

These are inserted into the vagina before sex where they cover the cervix and prevent sperm from reaching the uterus. The diaphragm and cervical cap, made of thin rubber, are used with a spermicide (*see below*), which increases the effectiveness of the method by killing any stray sperm. Both are left in place for several hours and are reusable after cleaning.

Spermicidal sponge

EMERGENCY CONTRACEPTION

Contraceptives can sometimes fail. Emergency contraception is available from a doctor if action is taken quickly. One option is the emergency, or morning-after, pill. This must be taken within 72 hours of unprotected intercourse. The second option is to have an IUD fitted by a doctor within five days of unprotected sex. Such emergency methods must not be relied on as a regular contraceptive, however.

Pessaries containing
spermicide

Spermicidal
film

SPERMICIDES

These create a chemical barrier that kills or disables sperm in the vagina, so that the sperm don't reach the uterus. They are not an effective contraceptive on their own, however: they must always be used with another contraceptive, such as a cervical cap or diaphragm, to be effective. The spermicide is put into the vagina before intercourse. There are six main types: the spermicidal sponge which is inserted into the vagina rather like a cap; pessaries and film, which melt inside the vagina; foam, which is squirted into the vagina; and creams and gels, which are used on diaphragms or cervical caps, or are squeezed into the vagina with a special applicator.

OTHER METHODS

There are other methods of contraception that are not recommended for young people. The intrauterine device, or IUD (*see page 66*), is a small piece of plastic with copper wire wrapped around it. It is inserted inside the uterus by a doctor, and prevents sperm from reaching the egg or a fertilized egg from settling. The IUD is not usually a first choice for young women who have not had children, because of the risk of infection. Sterilization operations (*see page 67*) permanently prevent women from becoming pregnant, or men from releasing sperm. Natural methods of contraception (*see page 67*) rely on knowing when the woman is fertile each month, and using other methods of contraception or abstaining at that time.

IUD

Spermicidal foam

Spermicidal cream

Applicator used with spermicide

Hormonal methods

Because these contraceptives contain synthetic drugs that alter a woman's hormonal cycle, they are available only on prescription. If you choose to use any of the hormonal methods, you will be asked to see a doctor regularly to have a general check-up.

RELIABILITY

Hormonal methods are 99 percent effective if they are used carefully. Effectiveness of the combined pill is reduced with less careful use. Used carefully, the progestogen-only pill is only slightly less reliable than the combined pill. Injectable contraceptives are nearly 100 percent effective for the stated length of time – Depo-Provera up to 12 weeks and Noristerat up to 8 weeks. (These injectable hormones are not approved for contraception in Australia and they are not generally recommended in New Zealand.) Implants are nearly 100 percent effective.

WHAT IS THE PILL?

There are two basic types of pill. The combined pill contains low doses of the hormones oestrogen and progestogen. This prevents ovulation (*see page 16*) so conception cannot take place. The progestogen-only pill contains progestogen. This pill causes the cervix to produce thick mucus, preventing sperm from entering the uterus; it may also prevent ovulation.

THE COMBINED PILL

The combined pill is taken each day for 21 days, followed by a seven-day break before starting the next pack. During the break some bleeding occurs. Women who like to take their pills without a break can have the every-day pill. Each pack contains 28 pills, but the last seven pills contain no hormones. Bleeding occurs while these inactive pills are being taken.

ADVANTAGES AND DISADVANTAGES

The combined pill can be taken by most women, and it usually makes periods lighter and less painful. Because it is so reliable, the pill largely removes the fear of becoming pregnant, and helps many women and their partners feel more relaxed about sex. Before prescribing a contraceptive pill, a doctor will ask about a woman's health and that of her immediate family. This is because the pill may not be suitable for a woman if she, or members of her family, suffer from certain health problems such as high blood pressure. It is also not suitable for smokers over 35, or very overweight women. Some women suffer side effects such as headaches, or weight gain. If these do not go away, the woman should consult her doctor. Certain medication and a severe stomach upset - vomiting or severe diarrhoea - can prevent the pill from working, and should be treated as a missed pill (*see opposite*).

THE PROGESTOGEN-ONLY PILL

The progestogen-only pill must be taken at the same time every day, without a break between packs. It is therefore not suitable for people who tend to be forgetful.

ADVANTAGES AND DISADVANTAGES

The progestogen-only pill may cause periods to be irregular or missed – this is normal, but it should be mentioned to the doctor at a check-up. It is also suitable for women who cannot take oestrogen. If taken more than three hours late, however, its effectiveness may be lost, and any vomiting or severe diarrhoea will also stop it from working. Other methods of contraception would need to be used in this case.

THE INJECTABLE CONTRACEPTIVE

Progestogen is injected into the buttock and is released into the body over the following weeks. It works by preventing the release of an egg from the ovary each month. Injections are needed every eight or 12 weeks. There are two types of injection – Depo-Provera, which lasts for up to 12 weeks, and Noristerat, which lasts up to eight weeks.

Injectable contraception allows sex to be spontaneous and relieves the pressure of worrying about taking pills. The disadvantages are that possible side effects such as weight gain or irregular bleeding may be with you until the drug wears off. Bleeding can be heavy at first, but most women have no bleeding after the second injection.

HORMONAL IMPLANTS

This is a fairly new method of hormonal contraception. Implants are plastic tubes, each tube about 34 mm (1 ¼ in) long and thinner than a matchstick, containing progestogen. Six tubes are inserted under the skin of a woman's upper arm. This is done under local anaesthetic by a doctor, and takes about 10 minutes. The implant releases a constant supply of progestogen straight into the bloodstream for five years. Its effect can be reversed at any time by removing the tubes. Any side effects are the same as those for the progestogen-only pill.

MEMORY AID

To help you to remember to take your pill every day you should adopt a set routine. Always take it on waking or on going to bed at night. Follow the instructions and carry your pills with you in case you stay away for a night.

I told my girlfriend I didn't like her being on the pill, because it means that she could sleep with anyone. She told me I was being stupid.

David, 18 years

IF YOU FORGET A PILL

Act right away
Combined pill
If the pill is over 12 hours late, use another contraceptive method for the next seven days. If there are fewer than seven pills left in the pack, use another method for the next seven days, and start the next pack as soon as you finish this one. If you use the every-day pill, throw away the pack with its remaining inactive pills, start a new one right away on the active pills, and use another method for the next seven days.
Progestogen-only pill
If you are more than three hours late, use another contraceptive method for the next seven days.

QUESTIONS AND ANSWERS

Because I have painful periods, my doctor is going to put me on the pill. Is this a good idea?
Tracey, 14 years

Your doctor wouldn't prescribe the pill if you are likely to suffer any harmful side effects. Although you are on the contraceptive pill, this doesn't mean that you have to become sexually active right away. The pill is being prescribed to relieve your symptoms.

I am on the pill but I don't have one steady sexual partner, so I want to use a condom to prevent any infection. What should I say to my partner?
Janine, 18 years

It is a good idea to insist on using a condom while you are still experimenting with relationships. Tell your partner that using a condom is a protection of your own and his health.

Condoms

Both male and female condoms are easy to obtain and reliable if used properly. They can help to prevent not only pregnancy, but also the spread of sexually transmitted infections, including HIV. They also reduce the risk of cervical cancer in women *(see page 79)*.

THE MALE CONDOM

The male condom is usually made of very thin latex rubber, and fits snugly over the erect penis. When a man comes, or ejaculates, his semen stays inside the condom. In some countries condoms are made from animal tissues and are sold as a luxury item because they are supposed to "feel more natural". They are not effective enough to protect against pregnancy or infection. Condoms are also known by other names, including sheaths, rubbers, French letters, and johnnies.

Male condoms can be bought in pharmacies and supermarkets, and can be obtained from family planning clinics and some doctors. They come in different shapes and colours, with or without a teat at the end, and even in different flavours. Many are lubricated with spermicide to make them easier and safer to use. Whichever type of condom you choose, check that it is not past its expiry date, and that it conforms to current national or international safety standards.

THE FEMALE CONDOM

The female condom is a fairly new barrier method that can be bought in pharmacies or obtained from some family planning clinics. It is a plastic tube that is bought ready lubricated; it fits inside the vagina, where it forms a lining into which the man directs his penis. One end is closed, and contains a ring to help keep it in place. The other end is held open with a similar ring that lies outside the vagina.

During sexual intercourse, when the woman's partner ejaculates inside her vagina, his semen is trapped inside the condom so that the sperm are prevented from swimming through the cervix and into her uterus.

BUYING AND USING CONDOMS

You may feel embarrassed about buying condoms at first, but you can pick them off supermarket shelves and shop assistants are used to selling them every day to people of all ages. There are many types of condoms to try – they are sold in many different brands and types.

RELIABILITY

Female condoms are a relatively new method of contraception. They are thought to be as reliable as male condoms. Male condoms are between 85 and 98 percent effective, depending on care taken in handling them.

USING LUBRICANTS

Some couples prefer to use extra lubrication with condoms. Only spermicide creams or special gels should be used with male condoms. Products containing oil, such as baby oil, body lotions, and Vaseline, must *not* be used, because they can damage the rubber and make the condom leak. Female condoms are made of plastic, so any lubricants can be used with them.

USING A MALE CONDOM

The male condom is a convenient method of contraception. Putting on a condom need not be embarrassing and inconvenient. It can be part of the fun of foreplay if you do it together.

Do not remove the condom until the penis has withdrawn from the vagina. Check it for any leakage and discard carefully after use – if possible, not down the toilet. Do not re-use.

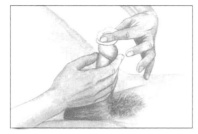

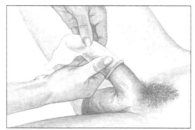

1 Whether you have a condom with or without a teat, squeeze the end to push out the air, so that there is space left for the sperm.

2 When the penis is erect, unroll the condom over the penis to the base. Doing this together can be fun.

3 After ejaculation, the man holds the condom on his penis. Once he withdraws from the vagina, it can be taken off and discarded carefully.

USING A FEMALE CONDOM

The female condom is a fairly recent contraceptive. It is strong and comes ready lubricated. It also allows the woman to take the responsibility for safer sex. Check for any leakage and discard carefully after use.

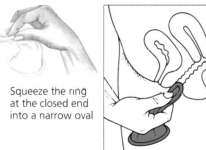

Squeeze the ring at the closed end into a narrow oval

1 Remove the condom from the packaging – it is already lubricated – and, with one hand, spread the labia (*see page 14*). With the other hand, slide the squeezed ring of the condom into your vagina, pushing it as far as you can.

To insert the female condom, find a comfortable position to relax your vagina

2 Put your finger inside the condom and manoeuvre the ring up past the pubic bone. The ring doesn't have to cover the cervix like a diaphragm does (*see page 64*). When in place, it should hang down about 5 cm (2 in) outside your vagina.

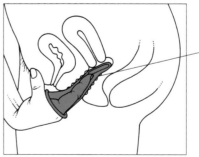

Push the closed end up into your vagina

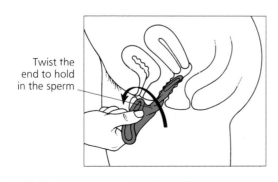

Twist the end to hold in the sperm

3 After sex when the man's penis has been withdrawn, twist the open end of the condom to seal in the sperm. Pull the whole condom out of your vagina. Check the sheath for any leakages before you discard it. Do not use it again.

Other methods

There are other contraceptive options that are available. These include intrauterine devices, permanent sterilization, and natural methods. Emergency contraception is used specifically and sparingly, not as a regular method.

THE INTRAUTERINE DEVICE (IUD)

Most IUDs (previously known as the coil) are pieces of plastic, 2–4 cm (1–1½ in) long, wound with copper wire. The IUD works mainly by preventing sperm from reaching the egg, or rarely, by preventing a fertilized egg from settling in the uterus. The IUD is inserted into the uterus by a doctor using a special instrument. It can stay there for five years and is removed by a doctor.

An IUD is not chemical, it doesn't interfere with sexual intercourse, and it is effective as soon as it is fitted. However, IUDs may increase the risk of sexually transmitted infection in the uterus or the fallopian tubes – infection that could lead to infertility. This is one reason why they may not be recommended for young women who are not in a mutually faithful relationship. Periods can be heavier and it is possible for the IUD to become dislodged; it should be checked regularly by feeling for the tail of threads at the cervix (*see left*).

RELIABILITY

The IUD is more than 98 percent reliable. Sterilization for women is nearly 100 percent reliable once a woman has had her first period after the operation, and, for men, within a few months – the time it takes for the sperm to be cleared from the tubes. Natural methods are about 80 to 98 percent effective if used properly.

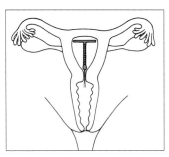

THE IUD IN PLACE
Two fine threads attached to the base of the IUD project a short way into the vagina. The woman can check, by putting a finger in her vagina and feeling for the threads, that the IUD is still in place.

EMERGENCY CONTRACEPTION

Emergency or post-coital (after intercourse) contraception, also known as the morning-after pill, is used when a woman thinks she is at risk of an unplanned pregnancy soon after intercourse. The reason could be forgetting to use contraception, an accident such as a condom tearing or slipping off, or that a woman was not planning to have sex – this includes sexual assault and rape. If you think you are at risk you should contact your doctor or family planning clinic within 72 hours of the unprotected intercourse. You will probably be given two special pills to take immediately, and another two to take 12 hours later. The pills alter a woman's hormonal balance, which delays ovulation or prevents implantation. They can make you feel sick. If you vomit within three hours, you may need to take more pills. This method is about 95 to 99 percent effective.

Another method in emergencies is to have an IUD fitted, which can be done up to five days after unprotected intercourse. This prevents the egg from embedding itself in the uterine lining. The IUD can be removed when the next period starts. This is almost 100 percent effective in preventing pregnancy and is chosen if the time limit for the hormonal method has passed or the woman cannot take oestrogen.

STERILIZATION

Male sterilization, or vasectomy, is done by cutting the sperm duct, or vas deferens *(see page 25);* this prevents sperm from reaching the penis. Female sterilization is done by cutting or blocking the fallopian tubes *(see page 15),* preventing eggs from reaching the uterus. Neither affects the person's interest in, or ability to enjoy, sex. A man still ejaculates semen (without the sperm) and a woman still has periods. These operations are designed to be irreversible. Doctors generally sterilize only men or women over 30 who have completed their family.

NATURAL METHODS

Natural methods depend on careful monitoring of a woman's cycle, finding out when she is fertile by working out when she ovulates *(see pages 16-17).* During the fertile part of the cycle, other barrier forms of contraception should be used or you can abstain from penetrative sex. To be effective the methods must be taught by a trained teacher and not tried without instruction. You need to become familiar with your menstrual cycle and remember that day 1 is the first day of bleeding.

TAKING TEMPERATURES

Temperature changes, measured with a fertility thermometer at the same time each day before getting out of bed (either orally, rectally, or vaginally), show when a woman is fertile. The fertility thermometer has a narrow range of temperatures, making it easy to read. Immediately after ovulation, the body temperature drops a little and then rises by between 0.2°C and 0.4°C. It remains at this temperature until the next period.

My friend had sex without using a contraceptive. She asked me if she could take some of my pills to stop her getting pregnant. I said it wouldn't work, and she should see her doctor.

Tracey, 17 years

USING THE NATURAL METHOD

You will need to keep a daily record in chart form of your temperature and/or cervical mucus for this method. Day 1 is the first day of bleeding. Depending on the length of your cycle, ovulation should occur 12-16 days *before* the next period is due.

This chart is based on an average 28-day cycle.

At ovulation mucus resembles the white of an egg

I didn't believe him when he said that he could pull out in time. I had a condom with me, just in case.

Marianne, 18 years

CERVICAL MUCUS METHOD

Changes in the consistency of a woman's cervical mucus *(see page 17)* also indicate ovulation. You can stretch a little vaginal discharge between your thumb and index finger to see the colour and consistency. Immediately after your period you may not notice much cervical mucus. After a few days your cervical mucus may be more noticeable as a discharge; it is thick, sticky, and cloudy. As you are about to ovulate and after you have just ovulated, there is more mucus, and it is clear and stretchy – like raw egg white. When it changes back to being thick and cloudy, this is a safe time. With care, the temperature and mucus methods can be very reliable.

ADVANTAGES AND DISADVANTAGES

Natural family planning has been practised for centuries, and it has no known side effects. Both the man and woman need to be involved and be prepared to use barrier methods or abstain at other times to be sure. It does require a detailed knowledge of a woman's cycle and this record keeping is time-consuming and must be precise. Good teaching is important if this method is to be effective.

"BEING CAREFUL" OR COITUS INTERRUPTUS

Coitus interruptus or withdrawal is when the man withdraws his penis from the vagina just before orgasm. This is not at all reliable as birth control because some sperm can leak before ejaculation; one sperm is all that is necessary for a pregnancy. Other disadvantages are that this is a difficult thing to do in practice, and the experience for both partners can be frustrating and unsatisfactory.

QUESTIONS AND ANSWERS

What if I were sterilized now and have it undone when I am older and want a family?
Kenny, 16 years

When you are young, a doctor would be very unlikely to consider sterilization unless your health were at risk. If you are sterilized, complicated surgery is required to reverse the sterilization operation. After sterilization, you are still exposing yourself and your partner to sexually transmitted infections *(see pages 80-83)* if you never use any other form of contraception such as a condom.

I've heard that if you shake up a bottle of warm cola or any carbonated drink, and squirt it up into your vagina after you have sex, it will stop you from getting pregnant because it washes all the sperm back out. Is this true?
Lucy, 15 years

No, this will not prevent you from becoming pregnant. Washing out the vagina like this is called douching. By the time you start douching after you've had sex, the sperm will already be swimming into the uterus. Douching after sex can cause irritation or an infection in your vagina.

PREGNANCY AND BEING A PARENT

How pregnancy starts

Childbirth

Unplanned pregnancy

How pregnancy starts

The moment of fertilization, when egg and sperm fuse together, is the most significant event in the whole reproductive process. All the material is there for a new individual, who inherits genes from both parents.

About every 28 days – although it can actually be anywhere between 21 and 42 days – from puberty to menopause, an egg, or ovum, is released from a woman's ovaries *(see page 15)*. If she has intercourse around this time, there is a good chance that her partner's sperm will meet and fertilize the egg, beginning the process of conception. The process is complete when the ball of cells that develops from the fertilized egg attaches itself to the wall of the uterus. At first this implanted mass of cells is called an embryo. Some of the cells develop into the placenta, which anchors the embryo in the uterus wall and delivers nutrition from the mother. A cushioning bag of fluid, called the amniotic sac, forms around the embryo. Eight weeks after fertilization, the embryo has a recognizable form, with face and limbs and all its major organs. It is now called a fetus. The baby will be born about 40 weeks after the first day of the woman's last period.

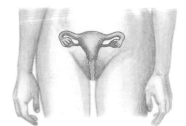

EXPANSION OF THE UTERUS
The uterus is about 10 cm (4 in) long, and 8 cm (3 in) wide. In pregnancy, its capacity and muscle bulk increase until it is about 38 cm (15 in) long and 25 cm (10 in) wide.

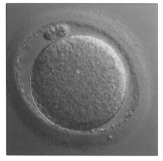

Hundreds of sperm surround the ripe egg, all trying to break through. The sperm release an enzyme, which dissolves the covering of the egg so that one sperm eventually penetrates it. Once this happens, no other sperm can get through. The fertilized egg, called a zygote, has 46 chromosomes – 23 from the sperm and 23 from the egg.

BOY OR GIRL?

A baby's gender depends on the sperm. Genetic information, including sex, is carried in chromosomes – there is an identical set of 46 of these in every cell of the body, but eggs and sperm have only 23 each. Sperm can carry either an X or a Y chromosome. The egg only carries an X chromosome. If a Y sperm fertilizes an egg, the baby's cells will be XY, and it will be a boy. If the sperm is X, the baby's cells will be XX, and it will be a girl.

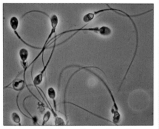

A sperm's head carries the genetic information, and its long tail propels it.

QUESTIONS AND ANSWERS

Can a girl get pregnant the first time she has sex?
Nathan, 13 years

Yes: whether it's the first time or the twenty-first, she can get pregnant if the couple don't use contraception.

If a girl misses a period, is she definitely pregnant?
Joely, 14 years

No. Girls often have irregular periods, so being late, or even missing a period, is not uncommon. The only reliable way to find out is to have a pregnancy test *(see page 75)* if pregnancy is a possibility.

A pregnancy test is able to detect a certain hormone in a woman's urine. This is usually possible within a week of a missed period. However, whatever the result, it is advisable to visit a doctor or clinic to have the result confirmed.

A friend told me that you can't get pregnant if you have sex during your period – is she right?
Ashley, 15 years

No. Ovulation can happen shortly after a period, and sperm can live to find an egg for up to three days, so a girl certainly can become pregnant if she has sex during her period.

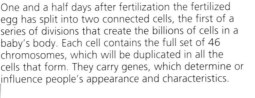

One and a half days after fertilization the fertilized egg has split into two connected cells, the first of a series of divisions that create the billions of cells in a baby's body. Each cell contains the full set of 46 chromosomes, which will be duplicated in all the cells that form. They carry genes, which determine or influence people's appearance and characteristics.

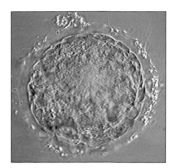

Three days after fertilization more cell divisions have produced a solid mass of 64 separate cells. This ball of cells, which is called a morula, is no bigger than the full stop at the end of this sentence. It is still travelling down the fallopian tube, and will not reach the uterus for another 24 hours.

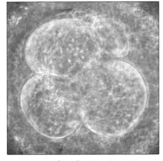

Fallopian tube

Two days after fertilization the journey down to the uterus continues. A second split has taken place, producing four cells. From now on, the cells will divide about twice every day.

Thickened by hormones, the uterine lining is ready to receive the egg

An egg has around 12-24 hours in which to be fertilized after ovulation

Ovary

THE STAGES OF CONCEPTION

During intercourse *(see pages 46-47),* up to 500 million sperm are released from the penis. The sperm swim into the uterus and towards the ovaries – only a few thousand will make it this far. If they find an egg, they will surround it, and there is a good chance that one of them will fertilize it. The fertilized egg divides into a mass of cells as it travels down the fallopian tube. It attaches itself to the inside of the uterus, and at this site, the placenta begins to grow. The uterus keeps its lining, which is usually shed in menstruation, so the first sign of pregnancy is normally a missed period. Over the next 266 days, the tiny ball of cells develops at a rapid rate into a fully formed baby.

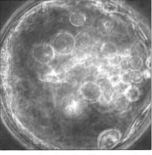

One week after fertilization a hollow space has formed in the centre of the ball of cells, now called a blastocyst. After floating in the uterus for two or three days, it starts to embed itself in the wall. When the blastocyst is fully implanted, conception is complete.

Childbirth

After about 40 weeks, a pregnancy comes to an end when the baby is born. The sequence of events that leads to the birth is called labour – divided into three stages – during which the uterus contracts with increasing strength and pushes the baby and placenta out.

DEPRESSION

Many new mothers feel helpless and have crying spells after giving birth. This is caused by sudden changes in the hormone levels and the feeling of anti-climax after birth; it is sometimes called "baby blues". If this feeling persists, and the mother is still feeling depressed four weeks after the birth, she should see a doctor as she could be suffering from post-natal depression.

Regular contractions of the uterus are a sign that labour has begun. It is time to contact the hospital to arrange to go in for the birth. At the hospital, a midwife carries out routine checks during the first stage of the labour. The father or a close friend or relative is usually present throughout. Contractions of the uterus increase in frequency and intensity. The woman can feel tired, and frightened at this time. She may experience extreme pain, although procedures learned at antenatal classes or pain-killing drugs will help lessen the pain, and reduce fear. The support and encouragement of those with her is very important. During the second stage of labour the baby is born, the midwife assesses its health and hands the baby to the mother.

Returning home can be a terrific let-down. After all the congratulations comes the responsibility of taking care of the new arrival. Parents may feel exhausted from lack of sleep, and mothers in particular can feel lonely and isolated during the first months. Support from a partner, family, and friends is important at this time. It can also be helpful and reassuring to meet other young parents to share ideas and solve problems.

DEVELOPMENT OF THE FETUS

At 16 weeks, the mother will notice changes to her breasts. The fetus has started to move. Its heartbeat can be heard. By 20 weeks, the mother begins to look pregnant and she can feel the fetus moving inside her. At 32 weeks, the fetus is completely formed and if born now, it has a 50 percent chance of survival. In the remaining 8 weeks it will put on fat, becoming plumper and less wrinkled.

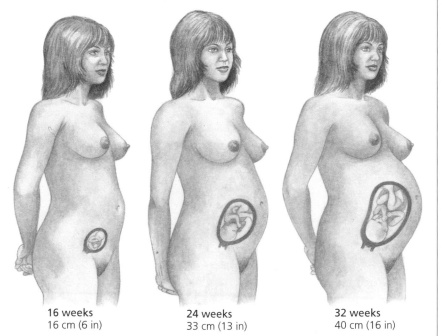

16 weeks
16 cm (6 in)

24 weeks
33 cm (13 in)

32 weeks
40 cm (16 in)

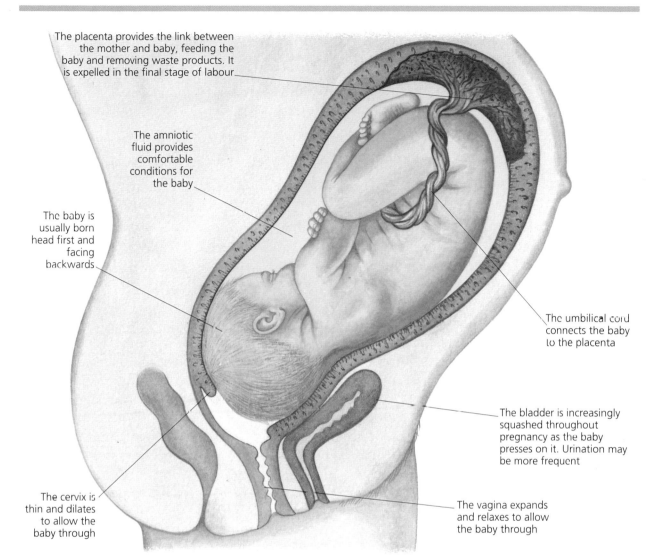

The placenta provides the link between the mother and baby, feeding the baby and removing waste products. It is expelled in the final stage of labour

The amniotic fluid provides comfortable conditions for the baby

The baby is usually born head first and facing backwards

The umbilical cord connects the baby to the placenta

The bladder is increasingly squashed throughout pregnancy as the baby presses on it. Urination may be more frequent

The cervix is thin and dilates to allow the baby through

The vagina expands and relaxes to allow the baby through

THE PELVIC GIRDLE

During birth, the baby has to pass through a narrow opening in the pelvic girdle, a ring of bone consisting of the hip bones and lower spine, held together by tough ligaments. In fact, the baby is only able to squeeze through the narrow opening because hormones, released throughout pregnancy, relax the ligaments, making the pelvic girdle wider and more flexible so that it "gives" as the baby is born.

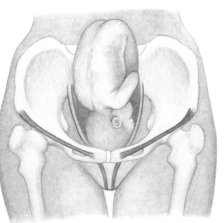

This is a front view of the baby's position in the pelvic girdle, with the uterus left out for clarity.

READY FOR THE BIRTH

Labour has three stages. The first stage generally lasts between 12 and 14 hours. The uterus contracts strongly and frequently. The bag of fluid surrounding the baby bursts, and the cervix opens up (dilates) to allow the baby's head to pass through. The cervix should be fully dilated before the second stage begins. This lasts about one hour. As the woman pushes downwards and her uterus contracts more strongly, the baby is born. After delivery, the umbilical cord is clamped and cut. During the final stage, which lasts about 15 minutes, the placenta is pushed out of the uterus.

Unplanned pregnancy

It's easy to think that this can't happen to you but it can be devastating to find out that it has. Once you are pregnant, it may be hard to think of anything except how you are going to tell your parents, but there are many other decisions you will also need to make.

FACING UP TO BEING PREGNANT

If you discover that you are pregnant, you may feel frightened, angry, and fearful about your future. The first step is to think through your feelings about the pregnancy, the baby, and what the future holds. It is very important that you act quickly to seek help and advice.

The choices facing you as a pregnant girl are not easy. You should not be pressured into doing what someone else thinks is right. Whatever choice you make, it has to be right for you. Your partner may want to share in the decisions, but might not be ready for the responsibility, or be much help. He may be another complication in your life right now. He may not want to know. In the end, what happens must be your choice. Your partner's agreement is not legally necessary for the continuation or termination of a pregnancy. Once a baby is born, if your partner's name is on the birth certificate, he has legal rights and responsibilities which may include financial support for you and the baby.

TELLING YOUR PARENTS

Depending on what you decide to do, you need support and advice, especially in making the decision about telling your parents. Even in the closest families this can be difficult. It may help to take a trusted family member or friend into your confidence so that they can help to smooth your path. If you really can't face telling your parents, the best place to turn to is a family planning clinic, health advisory centre or counselling service (*see pages 92-93*). The people there are trained to offer help and advice; they won't judge you or criticize you.

IF YOU CHOOSE TO HAVE THE BABY

If you are in a stable relationship, or have family willing to help and support you, you might keep the baby. This would mean rethinking your whole future. Babies are not

---

WHAT TO DO FIRST

To help you to sort out your feelings about the pregnancy, ask yourself the following questions first:
- Do you want the baby?
- Will your parents be supportive of your decision?
- Do you want your partner to be involved?
- Do you think your partner will stand by you?
- Is there someone you can confide in?
- Would you consider an abortion?
- Would you consider adoption?

BEING TOGETHER Once the baby is born, you will probably find that you can cope as well as women twice your age, and that you enjoy motherhood.

babies for long: try to imagine how you will feel bringing up a child for the next 16 or so years. If you are very young, or on your own, this will be even more difficult. The opportunity to continue your schooling and gain qualifications will depend to a large degree on your family and how they support you both – whether financially or with accommodation – and on support from your school or education authority.

Having the baby and giving it up for adoption is another option. It is difficult to know how you will feel when the baby is actually born: some mothers find that they cannot give the baby up. Others go through with it, although they often change their minds once the process is under way.

Once your pregnancy starts to show, you may want to leave school or be asked to go. You can make arrangements to continue with your education until the birth. If you know you want to continue your studies after the baby is born, you may find that your family can help to arrange some form of childcare, or there may be an educational unit in your area for young mothers and their babies. Such facilities are not nationwide and depend on where you live.

BEING A LONE PARENT

Bringing up a child alone is not easy. It can be harder still if all your friends are still carefree teenagers. Money and housing are often a problem. If your family are behind you, this can make an enormous difference. They may be able to help you out financially, but, just as importantly, they can give you emotional support and practical help so that you don't feel quite as much out on your own. Even if your parents are upset or angry about an unexpected pregnancy, it is worth trying to build bridges and maintain a good relationship with them.

HAVING THE PREGNANCY TERMINATED

Abortion is the medical term for the termination of a pregnancy. It is a subject that raises many issues and most people have a view on whether it is an appropriate course of action or not. Remember, though, it is your choice if you decide to end your pregnancy.

The earlier an abortion is performed, the safer it is. A medical abortion avoids the need for an operation. This is not an easy option, however. It can only be done within 63 days of the first day of your last period and it involves three visits to the hospital or clinic. On the first visit three tablets are taken which stop the pregnancy. Two days later a pessary is inserted into the vagina. This causes the lining of the uterus and the pregnancy to be lost in the bleeding that follows. The final visit is to check that everything is okay.

The worst bit was telling mum and dad. Once I'd done that, it was easier to think clearly about what I wanted to do.

Marion, 16 years

PREGNANCY TEST

A variety of pregnancy testing kits are available from pharmacies. One type consists of a strip impregnated with chemicals. This is held in the woman's urine for a few seconds, and if it changes colour, she is pregnant. These kits are 99 percent accurate, but results should be confirmed by a doctor or at a clinic. There are a number of agencies that offer free pregnancy testing services and they can also give you advice about contraception if you are not pregnant (*see pages 92-93*).

SIGNS OF PREGNANCY

- A missed period.
- Tingling and tender breasts.
- A strange metallic taste in your mouth.
- Wanting to urinate more frequently.
- An increase in white vaginal discharge.
- Feeling tired.
- Suddenly craving or disliking certain foods.
- Nausea.

Up to 12 weeks abortion is normally done by vacuum or suction. Under general anaesthetic the cervix is dilated and the uterine lining is sucked out. This takes about 10 minutes. Between 12 and 16 weeks a method known as a D & E is used. This stands for dilatation and evacuation. Under general anaesthetic the cervix is dilated, and an instrument scrapes out the contents of the uterus.

After 16 weeks, premature labour is induced with a drug, causing a miscarriage. The drug is often in the form of a prostaglandin pessary inserted into the vagina against the cervix. The hormone stimulates the uterus to contract much as it does in labour. This can be upsetting because it is like a real birth, so the earlier the abortion is arranged, the better.

You might have strong views on whether or not you would have an abortion should you ever find that you were pregnant. But you could feel differently when you are actually pregnant, or your partner is. If you are thinking of having an abortion, or you aren't sure, see either your own doctor or a doctor at a family planning clinic as soon as possible so that you can make an informed decision.

THE AFTERMATH

After an abortion you may feel relieved, or you may not feel as pleased as you thought you would. It is easy to underestimate your sense of loss, even when you are convinced this way was the correct course of action. The best thing to do is to talk to someone sympathetic, such as a friend or a counsellor at a family planning centre. Don't bottle it up – seek support at this difficult time. It is also important to seek advice on the type of contraception to use in the future (*see pages 56-57*).

ABORTION LAW

The laws concerning whether abortion is legal or not differ widely. In the United Kingdom (except Northern Ireland) a woman can have an abortion up to 24 weeks. After that time, the pregnancy can only be terminated if there is serious risk to the woman's life or a fetal abnormality. However, an abortion will only be done as late as 24 weeks if there is serious risk to the woman's life. In Australia and New Zealand, abortion is only considered lawful if two doctors believe that the woman's physical or mental health is in danger. Parental consent may be necessary for those under 16.

QUESTIONS AND ANSWERS

My boyfriend's always been a bit wild. I would really like to have a baby with him. Do you think it would it settle him down?
Angela, 17 years

It's just as likely to make him leave. Have a baby when your relationship works, not to make it work.

I am pregnant, and I don't want to tell the baby's father because it is all over between us. My parents think I should. Is telling him the right thing to do?
Lee, 18 years

This is a difficult decision if your relationship is over but you have decided to keep the baby. If possible, your ex-boyfriend should really be told about the baby as he has his rights and responsibilities for the child (*see page 74*).

I think I'm pregnant. I still live at home: if I go to a clinic about it, will they tell my parents?
Tina, 16 years

No: whatever you tell a doctor or nurse at a clinic is confidential. If you are pregnant, it will be up to you to tell your parents.

SEX AND HEALTH

Looking after your body

Infections

HIV and AIDS

Looking after your body

In adolescence, your body changes in ways that affect not just your appearance, but your health and personal hygiene too. Your skin produces new smells, your genitals secrete new substances, and you have to start taking care of your body in a different way.

PERSONAL SCENT

Everyone has their own smell. If you are clean and healthy, it's natural and pleasant, and a part of you. Animals secrete scent chemicals called pheromones, which help to attract mates. It is possible that we secrete pheromones too, and that when we are attracted to someone, we may be responding to them by secreting these substances.

When body secretions have been exposed to air for a while, they become breeding grounds for bacteria and smell unpleasant. Almost everyone uses deodorants and anti-perspirants (*see page 10*) to counteract underarm odours. Daily washing of the genital area is also essential. A different, strong smell could be a sign of infection (*see pages 80-83*).

LUMPS AND BUMPS

With adulthood and changes in your shape, you will probably start to develop a new awareness of your body. Every now and again you can check for signs of anything different or out of the ordinary. For example, breasts normally feel uneven, and most breasts are larger than usual, and more lumpy and tender, before and during a period. You can get to know your breasts by checking them each month at the same time just after your

> *I hate it when people wear loads of perfume or aftershave – I always think they must be covering up some other smell. If you wash, you shouldn't need all that stuff.*
>
> Gurinder, 17 years

HAVING A SMEAR

You lie down on a flat surface with your knees bent and your feet together. You then let your knees drop to the side. The doctor or nurse inserts a speculum into your vagina. This metal instrument holds the vaginal walls apart while the examination is being carried out. It won't hurt, though it can feel cold and uncomfortable. A spatula is inserted through the speculum and scrapes cells from the cervix. You may not feel this. The sample of cells is put on a glass slide and sent away to a laboratory to be analysed. Your doctor will be notified about the result some weeks later by post. Keep a note in your diary so that you remember to have a further test in three years' time.

CHECKING THE TESTES

Testes should be examined regularly. The best time is just after a hot bath or shower, because the skin of the scrotum will be loose, making examination easy. Roll each testis between your thumb and fingers, gently moving the skin and feeling the entire surface. You are looking for changes in the texture, feel, size, and weight – the back of each testis is naturally lumpy (*see page 22*).

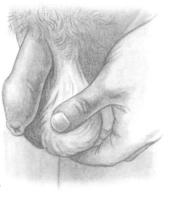

period. A painless lump or changes in skin texture are symptoms of one of the most common female cancers, though breast cancer is rare in young women. Early treatment improves the chances of successful treatment. If you note any changes or anything unusual, check with a doctor.

Cancer of the testes, while rare, is one of the most common cancers in young men. It can be cured if treated early. Regular checking is a good idea. If you have a painless lump or swelling that wasn't there before, see a doctor to set your mind at rest.

THE CERVICAL SMEAR TEST

This is a screening procedure for cervical cancer which is carried out regularly on sexually active women from the age of about 20, or within one to three years of having regular intercourse. This test is also known as a pap test. A doctor or nurse at a surgery or family planning clinic can do this. Abnormal cells on the cervix develop slowly and regular cervical smear tests allow these to be treated, usually with lasers. Cervical cancer has been linked to early sexual activity, genital warts, and smoking.

When my breasts first started, they were really lumpy, and I used to worry all the time that there was something wrong.

Chrissie, 15 years

CHECKING THE BREASTS

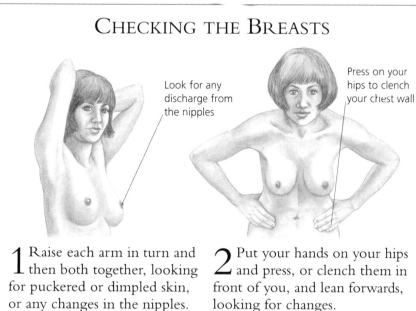

Look for any discharge from the nipples

Press on your hips to clench your chest wall

1 Raise each arm in turn and then both together, looking for puckered or dimpled skin, or any changes in the nipples.

2 Put your hands on your hips and press, or clench them in front of you, and lean forwards, looking for changes.

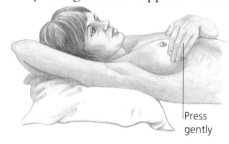

Press gently

3 While lying down, move your fingers over the surface of each breast. If you have large breasts, support them with the other hand. Feel for lumps and changes in skin texture.

PERSONAL HYGIENE ESSENTIALS

For girls
Wipe from front to back after a bowel movement, to avoid spreading germs forwards from the anus.
See your doctor if you have a different-smelling or coloured discharge: you might have an infection that could be treated *(see pages 80–83)*.
Don't use douches or vaginal deodorants: they are unnecessary and can irritate the vagina and cause infection.
Wash the vaginal area daily but avoid soaping between the vaginal lips, because soap may irritate the vulva.
Take regular baths or showers during your period.
For boys
If you are uncircumcised, pull your foreskin back to wash away the secretions (called smegma) that may accumulate underneath it.
Take regular baths or showers.
See your doctor if there is discharge from your penis.

Infections

If you are sexually active, you can pass on or pick up a sexually transmitted infection, so it is essential that you take precautions. Sex is never risk free, whether from an unplanned pregnancy or an infection, so you need to be responsible and practise safer sex to reduce the risk.

HOW DO YOU KNOW YOU'VE BEEN INFECTED?

Both sexes may have burning soreness or itching on or around the genitals, pain or discomfort when passing urine, or lumps, sores, blisters, or warts on or around the genitals. Men may have a clear or white discharge from the penis. Women's vaginal fluid may become heavier, change colour, or smell unpleasant. Women may need to urinate more frequently. Sometimes, however, women have no symptoms.

Infections that are not sexually transmitted can cause similar symptoms, and sometimes infections don't cause symptoms at all. So if someone you've had sex with tells you that they have an infection, you should visit a doctor or a clinic, even if you have no symptoms.

VISITING A CLINIC

Genito-urinary medicine clinics (GUM clinics) or sexually transmitted disease clinics (STD clinics) are usually part of a hospital complex; call your local hospital or health advisory centre to find out where the nearest one is (*see pages 92-93*). Anything you tell the staff is confidential, but part of their job is to try to stop infections spreading. They may ask you the names of your sexual partners, so that they can be contacted and treated. This can be done anonymously.

If you are worried about HIV (*see page 84*), staff can help you to decide whether to have a test. A test at a clinic is confidential. If your family doctor does the test, it goes on your medical files. You might one day need to give someone access to these, and not want them to know about the test.

WHAT HAPPENS AT A CLINIC?

At many GUM or STD clinics, you don't even need an appointment – you can walk in. The staff won't criticize you or give you a lecture. You will be examined and given tests, including a blood test. Once the infection is identified – some results are given straight away while others may take a few days – you will be given a course of treatment. Always finish any course of treatment, even if the symptoms go before the

---

" It was my first sexual experience and I was sure I'd got a sexually transmitted infection. It turned out to be just thrush and the pessaries cleared the itching up in 24 hours. "

Pippa, 16 years

SAFER SEX

■ Always use a condom to protect your own and your partner's sexual health.

■ Remember that a condom only reduces the risk, it doesn't eliminate it.

■ Casual sex or a lot of partners increases the chances of meeting someone with a sexually transmitted infection.

■ If a partner or ex-partner tells you they think they have an infection, seek medical advice, even if you have no symptoms.

■ Alcohol and drugs can make you less careful than you should be about sex and more inclined to take chances.

medication is finished, otherwise some germs may reinfect you. About half of the people who visit clinics have no infection.

WHY GO FOR TREATMENT?

With the exception of HIV *(see pages 84-85),* infections can be treated. Sometimes an infection does clear up by itself, but without treatment it can reappear. An untreated infection can also spread, causing permanent damage to both you and your partner's health, and you may pass it on to someone else in the meantime. Some infections can affect your chances of having children. Treatment is easiest if it is started early.

People who think they have caught a sexually transmitted infection often feel frightened or ashamed. They may feel too embarrassed to go to a clinic or see their doctor, but this is really not necessary. Doctors and clinics deal with these problems all the time, and will understand your feelings.

It can be difficult to tell someone that you have passed an infection on to them, or that you have an infection you could only have caught from them. But it is essential that your sexual partners know: they might have no symptoms and no idea that they have an infection. A clinic may be able to trace people for you and inform them anonymously.

I thought it was something really awful and I was seriously sick, but the clinic gave me antibiotics and it cleared up in a couple of weeks.

Craig, 16 years

SYMPTOMS

If you notice anything different around your genitals and you are sexually active, then you may have a sexually transmitted infection. Refer to the list of common infections and ailments that affect the sexual organs, overleaf. Common symptoms include:

- a white or different discharge from the penis – chlamydia, gonorrhoea, NSU
- itching around the genitals – genital herpes, pubic lice, thrush
- sore, itchy genitals – vaginitis, thrush
- pain when urinating – chlamydia, gonorrhoea, NSU
- lumps, sores, warts or blisters around the genitals – genital herpes, genital warts, syphilis
- a different discharge (frothy or yellow, for example) from the vagina – bacterial vaginosis, chlamydia, gonorrhoea, thrush, trichomoniasis, vaginitis

- an unpleasant smelly discharge – bacterial vaginosis, trichomoniasis
- frequent and/or painful urination – cystitis
- abdominal pain and tenderness – pelvic inflammatory disease

IF IN DOUBT

Practising safer sex *(see left)* is a way to reduce the risk of a sexually transmitted infection, but if you suffer any of the symptoms listed above, it is best to abstain from any sexual contact until you have visited your doctor or a clinic to find out whether there is a problem or not. About half of the people who visit clinics have no sexually transmitted infection.

VAGINAL DISCHARGE

It is normal to have some vaginal discharge – this is the way the vagina cleans and lubricates itself *(see page 14)*. Normally, this discharge is colourless and doesn't smell, although it dries to leave a yellow or brownish stain on underwear. If it begins to smell unpleasant, or looks different, perhaps frothy, this may indicate infection. Leaving a tampon in for too long can cause a foul-smelling vaginal discharge, and can also be dangerous *(see Toxic shock, page 64)*.

INFECTIONS AND IRRITATIONS

NAME	SYMPTOMS	TREATMENT
Bacterial vaginosis	A bacteria naturally present in women's bodies, it sometimes multiplies out of control and causes a greyish, frothy, fishy smelling discharge. Men can also have the germs, but usually without symptoms.	Antibiotic drugs or creams to insert into the vagina. If untreated, this infection may cause fertility problems.
Chlamydia	In men, pain on passing urine and a discharge from the penis. Women may have a vaginal discharge, or no symptoms. There may be pelvic pain during sex.	Antibiotics. If untreated, this could lead to infertility and other problems in women and men.
Cystitis	Frequent and painful urination, maybe only a trickle, which may smell strong and contain traces of blood. This is an infection of the bladder by bacteria that are naturally present in the body. Cystitis is common in women because a woman's urethra is short and the bacteria are able to reach the bladder from the rectum (see page 15). If a woman has strenuous sexual intercourse, this can set up mechanical stress resulting in cystitis (known as "honeymoon cystitis"). Men have a longer urethra, so cystitis in men is rare.	Self-treatment includes drinking plenty of water (with a teaspoon of bicarbonate of soda added to each glass) at the first sign of the symptoms to keep your urine flowing; about two glasses of liquids every hour. If symptoms do not disappear or you are uncomfortable, your doctor may prescribe antibiotics.
Genital herpes	Tenderness, tingling, and itching of the genitals, followed by blisters, which may burst to form painful sores. There is often pain on urinating, and sometimes a feeling of illness and a raised temperature. This is caused by the herpes simplex II virus. It can be caught through intercourse and is different from the herpes simplex I virus that causes cold sores on the mouth. The first attack usually clears up in about two weeks, but the virus stays in the body and may lead to further attacks.	The virus cannot be killed, but antiviral drugs and painkillers help to heal sores and reduce pain during attacks. Sex must be avoided, or condoms used, during attacks.
Genital warts	Soft warts appear on and around the anus, the penis, or the entrance to the vagina and cervix. They may go undetected because they are small, or disappear of their own accord.	They are removed by repeated application of a lotion or by surgery, but they tend to recur. Any woman who has had them, or whose partner has had them, should be sure to have a regular cervical smear test (see page 78), because of the link between genital warts and an increased risk of cervical cancer.
Gonorrhoea	Men suffer from pain on passing urine and have a discharge from the penis. Women contract the disease more rarely, and the main female symptom is a vaginal discharge, but more than half of all women with gonorrhoea have no symptoms. This is one of the oldest known infectious diseases.	Antibiotics. If untreated the disease can cause infertility in men and women, so a woman whose partner has gonorrhoea must be checked, too.

NAME	SYMPTOMS	TREATMENT
Nonspecific urethritis (NSU)	This mostly affects men, who may have pain on passing urine or a discharge from the penis: these symptoms can be very mild, however. Women may have a slight vaginal discharge or, often, no symptoms. This is the most common sexually transmitted infection, called nonspecific because its cause cannot always be identified.	Antibiotics. If untreated, infections can cause serious complications such as a rare form of arthritis.
Pelvic inflammatory disease (PID)	This is an infection of the female reproductive system. Symptoms include abdominal pain and tenderness, often immediately after or during sex. Periods may become irregular and painful. There may also be fever, backache, and vomiting. It cannot be passed on to sexual partners, but it is often a result of an untreated infection such as chlamydia or gonorrhoea.	Antibiotics. If the woman has an IUD fitted, it should be removed if the infection does not respond to treatment.
Pubic lice	Blood-sucking, crablike creatures, the size of a pinhead, live in the pubic hair where they cause itching. Pubic lice are sometimes passed on by sharing bedding and towels, although usually by sexual contact.	The white, shiny eggs cannot be removed by normal washing: a special insecticide lotion should be used. Towels, clothes, and bedding must be washed in very hot water to prevent re-infection.
Syphilis	The first sign of syphilis is a painless, but very infectious, sore at the site of infection. This heals on its own in a few weeks, but the germs remain in the body and develop.	Antibiotics. If untreated, the disease will progress to cause a rash, mouth sores, and general aching.
Thrush (candidiasis, monoliasis)	A white, curdy discharge, itching, redness and swelling of the vulva, and soreness on passing urine. It is not caused by sexual contact, but by a yeast or fungus that is naturally present in the vagina and the mouth and gut. Usually, this does no harm, because other bacteria keep it under control, but it can sometimes multiply out of control. This can happen as a result of diabetes, or antibiotic treatment. A woman who has thrush can pass it on to her partners through sexual contact, although this is rare. The glans of the penis may become inflamed.	Antifungal creams and pessaries. Oral tablets are also available. Thrush thrives in warm and airless conditions, so if a woman has an attack, it is wise to wear cotton underwear and avoid tight trousers.
Trichomoniasis	A frothy, yellowish, foul-smelling vaginal discharge in women. Men may suffer symptoms similar to those for nonspecific urethritis, but often have no symptoms.	Antibiotics.
Vaginitis	Irritation and sometimes discharge. It can be caused by various bacteria, usually thrush, trichomoniasis or bacterial vaginosis. Allergies to spermicides or to scented soaps can also cause inflammation.	Antifungal or antibiotic drugs depending on the cause, or avoiding the cause of the irritation.

HIV and AIDS

HIV is a virus that causes the illness known as AIDS. Anyone can contract this virus through unprotected sexual intercourse with an infected person or using infected needles. It is estimated that around 12 million people worldwide have contracted HIV.

THE IMMUNE SYSTEM

The body has an immune system which is its defence against infection. However, if the human immunodeficiency virus (HIV) enters the body, the cells in the body's immune system are invaded and cannot destroy the virus. HIV stays alive within the cells of the immune system, and may lie dormant there for years. At present there is no known way to kill this virus once it enters the body. A blood test will detect HIV. If there is HIV, the person is said to be HIV positive. Being HIV positive does not make people ill. Someone with HIV may look and feel well, and stay this way for a long time – often for years. But they are infectious to others, and will be for the rest of their lives.

THE ONSET OF AIDS

When HIV is active, the infected cells in the immune system die, and the virus is released into the blood to infect other cells. As the immune system is weakened, the person loses weight, tires easily, and becomes more vulnerable to all sorts of infections, such as skin disorders, ulcers, thrush, and diarrhoea. Eventually, serious problems, such as herpes, tuberculosis, and cancer, develop.

When a person becomes ill in this way, they are said to be suffering from acquired immune deficiency syndrome, or AIDS. Once a person reaches this final stage of the disease, they usually die of a major infection within a year or two.

HOW DOES HIV SPREAD?

HIV is found only in bodily fluids, and of these only blood, semen, and vaginal fluids have been shown to transmit infection. The virus enters the body through a sore or cut in the skin, or an injection, or through the membranes that line the mouth, the vagina, or the anus. A baby can contract HIV from its mother through the placenta in the uterus, or possibly through breast milk after birth.

The virus cannot survive for long outside the human body. It is perfectly safe to live with someone who has HIV or

> *When my dad told me my uncle had HIV, I just couldn't believe it. I didn't know what to say to him at first, but he acted just the same, so I do, too.*
>
> Ben, 12 years

HOW HIV IS SPREAD

It can be spread by:
- Unprotected sex.
- Through a wound.

It cannot be spread by:
- Lavatory seats, showers, or swimming pools.
- Food, cutlery, crockery, or drinking fountains.
- Coughs, sneezes, sweat, tears, or saliva.
- Hugs, handshakes, or other non-sexual contact.
- Insect bites.

AIDS, to share their food, to use the same cutlery and crockery, to share their towels, to touch or hug them, and even to sleep in the same bed as them. It is not safe to have unprotected sex, or share toothbrushes, razors, or, in the case of drug users, hypodermic syringes, with anyone who is, or may be, HIV positive in case body fluids are exchanged.

THE SEARCH FOR A SOLUTION

There is no real cure for even the mildest virus, such as the common cold. In some cases, vaccination can prevent viral infection. However, once you have a virus, the infection usually has to run its course. Some drugs have been tried in the hope that they can slow down the progress of AIDS; however, the search still goes on for a cure.

The other area of research is the attempt to find a vaccine. Worldwide vaccination for smallpox wiped out the disease this century: if a vaccine against HIV can be developed, AIDS might also be overcome.

SAFER SEX

Everyone can avoid doing things that put them at risk. Many people have already changed their behaviour to reduce the risks of infection; many still take risks, however. While you can never completely eliminate the chances of catching any infection, you can do a lot to protect yourself against being infected by HIV.

Kissing – even wet or French kissing – touching, hugging, or mutual masturbation are safe. Oral sex is slightly more risky, because bleeding gums and mouth sores are quite common and can provide a point of entry for the virus (*see page 51*). Sexual intercourse is still the most common means of infection. There is a higher risk with anal intercourse, because the lining of the anus tears more easily than that of the vagina, providing a way in for the virus. The risk can be reduced during intercourse by wearing a condom (*see pages 60-62*).

MINIMIZING THE RISKS

Most people know that unprotected sex carries risks and the more sexual partners you have, the higher the chances that one of them is HIV positive. But even with people you know, there is a risk. Whatever risks your partner takes or has taken in the past, you are taking too. Anything that involves blood can be risky: drug addicts who inject drugs have contracted HIV. Addicts who share needles or use dirty needles are putting themselves at risk.

Everyone should avoid sharing items such as razors, and even toothbrushes – people often have mouth sores or minor

He made such a fuss when I asked him to wear a condom – you'd think I was asking him to come to bed in wellington boots. He wore it, though.

Debbie, 17 years

LIVING WITH HIV

Many people with HIV stay well for years. The people around them may never know that they are HIV positive. People who are ignorant about AIDS are often frightened and can be cruel, so people who are HIV positive may be happier if only those close to them know. If you know someone with HIV, you can still be their friend. Just treat them normally, not fussing over them too much, but remember that they may sometimes tire easily or get depressed. If they want to talk about it, encourage them, and listen sympathetically. If they don't want to talk about it, accept that, too.

PROTECTING YOURSELF

▩ Use condoms (*see pages 60-62*) to protect you and your partner's health.
▩ Talk about your past, and be honest.
▩ If either of you has done things that put you at risk, get an HIV test.
▩ Don't take drugs intravenously – if you do, don't share needles, but get clean ones from a clinic.
▩ Remember that drinking alcohol can make you less careful than you should be.

cuts on their gums without even being aware of them. Tattooing and ear-piercing could also carry a small risk if instruments are not sterilized: ask about the needles used (*see below*). Having a blood transfusion should no longer be dangerous because blood is now screened.

When the disease first appeared in the developed world, most of its victims were gay or bisexual men, so some people used to think that AIDS was a disease of gay men, but this is not true. This prejudice can encourage heterosexuals to think that they are safe. It is better to behave in ways that will reduce the risks for everyone rather than to imagine that if, for example, you are female or heterosexual, you are therefore unlikely to be infected.

HAVING AN HIV TEST

If you are worried about HIV and AIDS, you should talk to a special counsellor in a clinic or contact a special advice line (*see pages 92-93*). Many clinics will not test you without this counselling, because the implications of the test are greater than people imagine.

The test is *not* for AIDS: it determines whether you have antibodies to HIV in your blood. Usually, the antibodies appear within six weeks of infection, but they can take up to six months to show up, so you may test negative but be asked to return for another test in six months. During this time, you should not do anything that puts you or any partner at risk.

QUESTIONS AND ANSWERS

Someone told me I shouldn't have my ears pierced because I might get HIV from the needle they use. Can this really happen?
Nicky, 14 years

This could happen if an unsterilized needle was used, which might have been previously used on someone who had HIV or AIDS. The same is true for the needles used for tattoos and acupuncture. But if you go to a reputable jeweller or store, there should be no risk: their needles should be sterile, or they should be using disposable needles. Don't be embarrassed to ask about hygiene methods before you have the piercing done, and if you're not happy, go elsewhere.

What does an HIV test involve, and if there's no cure, what's the point in anyone taking it?
Pete, 16 years

A small blood sample is taken and tested. The results are available in a few days – in some clinics on the same day. If the result is positive, the person infected will need to take steps to avoid passing the virus on to anyone else. They can tell anyone who needs to know: their partner, and their doctor or dentist when necessary. Because it can take from six to eight weeks from the time of infection for the antibodies to appear, the test is usually not considered reliable until six months after exposure to the infection.

PROBLEM AREAS

Sex and the law
Child sexual abuse
Sexual harassment
Indecent assault

Sex and the law

Whatever happens to your body should only happen with your consent, and because you want it to happen. There are laws designed to protect people from abuse by others.

THE AGE OF CONSENT

The law protects children until they are old enough to make their own decisions about sex. The age at which you are considered old enough to do this is called the age of consent. If you are under the age of consent *(see page 44)* and someone has sex with you, even if you agree to it, they are committing an offence. The age of consent varies from country to country.

SEXUAL OFFENCES

Some behaviour is always against the law. Incest (sex between close relations such as a parent or an uncle or aunt) is always illegal, regardless of age. Anything that offends or harms others, such as sexual harassment *(see opposite),* or forcing someone to have intercourse or commit a sexual act against their will *(see page 91),* is also against the law.

PORNOGRAPHY

Pornography is any material designed to arouse the viewer sexually. Some people claim that naked people in daily newspapers are pornographic, while others claim that they are harmless. In most countries, the law allows some kinds of material, but bans others. Real "hard-core" porn shows sexual acts with violence and depicts its subjects as objects to be dominated or humiliated. In most countries such material is illegal.

Pornography has been shown to affect people's attitudes; it can change the way that we view other people. Real people are unlikely to be as willing or as adventurous.

PROSTITUTION

Prostitution is the sale of sex, by men or women. In most countries, it is either illegal, or made very difficult by laws that a prostitute cannot avoid breaking. Few of these laws protect the prostitute, who leads a dangerous life, exposed to the risks of HIV infection, and other sexually transmitted infections, and of violence. In some countries, prostitution is legal.

Child sexual abuse

Child sexual abuse is any activity in which children are used by other people for sexual pleasure. It includes not only intercourse, but any kind of sexual touching.

WHO ABUSES?

Usually the abuser is a friend of the family or a relation or someone known to the child. Sometimes a child is abused by a parent, a sibling, a step parent, or step brothers or sisters.

It is difficult to know exactly how many children are abused. When adults are questioned about their childhood, a large number (and twice as many women as men) say that they were abused. Thousands of children call telephone helplines every year to confide that they have been, or are being, sexually abused.

WHAT IS ABUSE?

If you're not certain about what someone is doing, and whether it is abuse or not, ask yourself these questions to help you to make up your mind. Does what is happening make you feel uncomfortable? Are you being sworn to secrecy so that nobody else knows about it? Are they doing it for their pleasure, with no regard for how you feel? Do they threaten you or ignore you if you try to stop them? Do they say that something bad will happen if you tell? If the answer to any of these questions is yes, then you are being abused.

WHAT SHOULD YOU DO?

Whoever is abusing you, try to tell someone what is happening. Even though you feel fearful about what will happen, telling someone is the best thing to do. This is easy advice to give, but it is often difficult to follow, especially if a member of your family is involved.

It is important for you to realize that when an adult abuses a child, it is *always* the adult's fault, *never* the child's. It may take time for you to summon up the courage to tell someone what is happening, but nothing is likely to change unless you do.

A parent is the best person to tell, if you can. If you can't, tell a grandparent or another close relative whom you trust, a friend, or a sympathetic teacher at school. Or you can call one of the telephone helplines *(see pages 92-93)* and talk in confidence to a specially trained counsellor. They can advise you on the next step to take.

WHAT HAPPENS NEXT?

If the police or social services are told that a child is being sexually abused at home, the first thing they must do is to make sure that the child is safe. If possible, the authorities will try not to break up the family or take the child away from home, but the adult involved may have to leave the area, at least for a time. This "breathing space" gives everyone a chance to decide what should be done for the best, to seek professional help for both the child and the abuser if possible.

The police have to decide whether to charge the person concerned or not. They must check on everyone's story and collect evidence. Sometimes they can't bring charges – this doesn't mean that a crime has not been committed. If they do, you may have to appear in court and give evidence. By telling someone you may have prevented the person from doing the same thing again.

Whatever happens next, you will have done the right thing by telling somebody. It may be a long time before everything settles down again and your life gets back to something like normal, but counselling can help to get you through this time.

Sexual harassment

This is unwanted pestering of a sexual nature. It doesn't have to be physical – comments, whistling, or obscene telephone calls are also sexual harassment.

WHAT TO DO ABOUT IT

Sexual harassment is not about attraction, it is about belittling someone. It is often done by people in positions of power. If you have been harassed, remember that it was not your fault. You are not alone: many people are harassed every day. Even if you are scared, don't keep it to yourself, but tell someone you trust. Sharing the upset will often make it feel better. Most harassment is illegal, so report incidents to someone in authority or the police so that the perpetrator can be caught.

If the sexual harassment happens at school, take the names of any witnesses, and tell a parent and a senior teacher. If your complaint is ignored, the education authority should be told; if the harassment involves a criminal offence, the police should be informed. If you feel justified, do not be persuaded to drop the matter.

WHISTLES AND COMMENTS

Harassment of this sort is common. You may feel angered and humiliated, but depending on where you are and who you are with, you can either try to ignore it – responding may encourage the harasser – or be assertive and tell the harasser that you don't accept this behaviour. If anything like this happens at school, report it. Students, and even teachers, sometimes comment on teenagers' physical development. If you don't like this, tell the person, and if they go on, report it. If someone makes unwanted sexual suggestions, tell them to stop, ask others if it has happened to them, and report it to someone in authority.

FLASHERS AND PEEPING TOMS

Flashers are men who expose their penises in public. Get away as fast as you can. In all cases, tell a parent or teacher and the police. Flashing is a crime.

Voyeurs are people who try to watch others when they are undressing or naked, or having sex. They are also known as "peeping toms". If you ever see someone spying on you, tell a parent, and report it to the police. Voyeurism is a crime.

UNWANTED TOUCHING

Crowded places, such as trains or buses, give some people the chance to touch or rub themselves against you. Draw attention to what is going on by loudly telling the offender to stop, and tell a parent or other adult as soon as you can. Contact the police: this kind of harassment is a crime.

OBSCENE TELEPHONE CALLS

Also called nuisance, or dirty, phone calls, these are upsetting and illegal. Callers may be silent, or ask intimate questions, or make sexual threats. If you receive an obscene call, put the phone down calmly – don't slam it down. Don't talk to the caller, and never give your name. Tell a parent,

and contact the police and the telephone company. Calls can usually be traced easily, so if the caller persists, they can be caught and prosecuted.

KERB CRAWLERS

Kerb crawlers are drivers who harass pedestrians by driving slowly behind them, sometimes making obscene suggestions. Ignore any comments and walk away from the car. If possible, memorize the number of the car and pass it on to the police. Kerb crawling is an offence.

Indecent assault

If someone forces you to have sex against your will, it is rape – whether you are a man or a woman. Other forms of sexual attack are known as indecent assault.

WHAT IS RAPE?

Rape is a frightening and horrible experience and often rape victims feel guilty, even though they have done nothing wrong. They may feel dirty, as though they have been somehow "spoiled". Because of these feelings, the first reaction may be to tell nobody, and to pretend that nothing has happened.

YOU MAY KNOW YOUR ATTACKER

Most rape victims know the person who rapes them. When a girl is raped by someone she knows, it is often called "date rape". Many such rapes happen at or after parties, when one (or both) of the people involved has had too much to drink. If the girl says no, and the boy insists, this is still rape. If she finally gives in, she may feel raped because she didn't want to do it, although the boy could claim that she had consented. There is sometimes a fine line, however, between date rape and sexual bad manners. Boys and girls often expect different things: each assumes that the other knows what they want (or don't want), but they can't read each other's signals. Girls have to learn to be clear about what they want, and to make it clear that they mean it when they say no. And boys have to accept and believe a no as readily as they would a yes.

What to do if you are raped

It isn't always easy to tell anyone let alone the police. You may be afraid of the person who raped you, or feel you won't be believed. But if you keep silent, it may be harder for you to get over what has happened. It also allows your attacker to go unpunished, and they may rape someone else. Tell your parents, a relative, or a close friend. They should report the rape to the police at once. You should be able to talk to a specially trained woman police officer, who will make it as easy for you to talk as she can.

Even if you feel that you just want to forget the whole thing, it is sensible to collect some evidence. Forensic evidence, such as tiny fragments of skin under your nails, can be vital in securing a conviction. It is important that you are examined, either by a police doctor or by your own doctor, within 24 hours of the rape. The doctor's report is essential evidence if the police are to prosecute your attacker.

It will help you if you can talk about it to someone else, especially someone who has had a similar experience. Contact a rape crisis centre or a telephone helpline about this *(see pages 92-93)*, or ask your doctor to refer you to a counsellor.

Useful addresses

Most of the organizations listed here have branches outside the main centres. Ring the telephone numbers given here to find out the telephone number and address of the branch in your town.

PREGNANCY AND CONTRACEPTION

British Agencies for Adoption and Fostering (BAAF)
11 Southwark Street
LONDON SE1 IRQ
Tel: 071 407 8800
Information on adoption and fostering.

British Pregnancy Advisory Service (BPAS)
Austy Manor
Wootton Wawen
SOLIHULL
West Midlands B95 6BX
Tel: 021 643 1461
A national network of clinics offering counselling, pregnancy testing and abortion. Look up under "Family planning" or "Pregnancy" in the Yellow Pages.

Brook Advisory Centres
233 Tottenham Court Road
LONDON WIP 9AE
Tel: 071 580 2991
Advice, help and information to young people (under 26) on personal relationships, contraception, abortion, and pregnancy. Also pregnancy tests. Many of the services are free.

Family Planning Association (FPA)
27-35 Mortimer Street
LONDON W1N 7RJ
Tel: 071 636 7866
The FPA runs a free information service and produces free leaflets on contraception.

Health Education Authority (HEA)
Information Service
c/o Health Promotion Information Centre
Hamilton House
Mabledon Place
LONDON WC1H 9TX
Tel: 071 383 3833
The Information Service can give you the address of the nearest Health Promotion Unit where you can get free HEA leaflets on many aspects of health education.

National Council for One Parent Families
255 Kentish Town Road
LONDON NW5 2LX
Tel: 071 267 1361
A national service offering free information for lone parents.

National Society for the Prevention of Cruelty to Children (NSPCC) Child Protection Helpline.
Tel: 0800 800500
A free 24-hour telephone helpline offering advice and information to young people. Ring this telephone number if you are being, or have been, sexually abused

Pregnancy Advisory Service (PAS)
11-13 Charlotte Street
LONDON W1P 1HD
Tel: 071 637 8962
Offers counselling, pregnancy tests, and abortion.

COUNSELLING

Association to Aid the Sexual and Personal Relationships of People with a Disability (SPOD)
286 Camden Road
LONDON N7 OBJ
Tel: 071 607 8851
Advice, information, and counselling to young people with a disability.

Childline
Freepost 1111
LONDON N1 OBR
Tel: 0800 1111
A free telephone counselling service for young people in trouble or danger. Contact Childline if you are being, or have been, sexually abused.

The Children's Legal Centre
20 Compton Terrace
LONDON N1 2UN
Tel: 071 359 6251

Equal Opportunities Commission
Overseas House
Quay Street
MANCHESTER M3 3HN
Tel: 061 833 9244
Advice if you are being sexually harassed or sexually discriminated against.

Friend
Tel: 071 837 3337 between 7.30 pm and 10.30 pm (London Friend)
A national advice and counselling service for anyone who is, or thinks they might be gay.

Information Service on Incest and Child Sexual Abuse
London
Tel: 081 852 7432

London Lesbian Line
Tel: 071 251 6911
A national advice and counselling service for anyone who is, or thinks they might be, a lesbian.

Youth Access
Magazine Business Centre
11 Newarke Street
LEICESTER LE1 5SS
Tel: 0533 558763
Young people's counselling service.

Liberty
National Council for Civil Liberties (NCCL)
21 Tabard Street
LONDON SE1 4LA
Tel: 071 403 3888

Relate
Herbert Gray College
Little Church Street
RUGBY CV21 3AP
Tel: 0788 573241
A national service offering counselling to people with marriage, relationship, or sexual problems.

Royal Scottish Society for the Prevention of Cruelty to Children
Melville House
41 Polworth Terrace
EDINBURGH EH11 1NU
Tel: 031 337 8539/8530

Samaritans

If you are feeling desperate of suicidal, you can ring the Samaritans. The telephone number of your local Samaritans is in the telephone book under "Samaritans" or in the front under "Useful Information".

Standing Conference on Drug Abuse (SCODA)

Waterbridge House
32–36 Loman Street
LONDON SE1 0EE
Tel: 071 928 9500
For help with a drugs problem.

MEDICAL CONCERNS

Body Positive

51b Pilbeach Gardens
LONDON SW5 9EB
Tel: 071 835 1045
Tel: 071 373 9124 (helpline)
HIV self-help group.

Herpes Association Helpline

Tel: 071 609 9061
A telephone helpline offering information about herpes.

National AIDS Helpline

Tel: 0800 567123
A national service offering free and confidential advice and information about HIV and AIDS 24 hours a day, seven days a week. If you are deaf or hard of hearing, ring Minicom on 0800 521361 every day from 10am to 10pm. The National AIDS Helpline is staffed with people who speak the following languages:
Bengali, Gujarati, Hindi, Punjabi, and Urdu on Wednesdays between 6pm and 10pm ring 0800 282445; Cantonese on Tuesdays between 6pm and 10pm, ring 0800 282446; Arabic on Wednesdays between 6pm and 10pm, ring 0800 282447 There is an answerphone service in these languages at other times and leaflets in these languages.

Positively Women

5 Sebastian Street
LONDON EC1V 0HE
Tel: 071 490 5515
A support agency for women living with HIV.

SEXUALLY TRANSMITTED INFECTIONS

If you suspect you have a sexually transmitted infection, it is important to get treatment as soon as possible. Ring your local hospital and ask for the GUM clinic. For information about AIDS testing contact the Terence Higgins Trust (below) or the department of genito-urinary medicine at your local general hospital.

Terence Higgins Trust

52–54 Grays Inn Road
LONDON WC1X 8JU
Tel: 071 242 1010 (helpline)
Telephone helpline giving advice and information about HIV and AIDS. Open from 3pm to 10pm.

SUPPORT AND COUNSELLING IN THE LONG TERM

Alternative Medical Centre

56 Harley House
LONDON NW1 5HW
Tel: 071 486 4115

TENDENCIES TO VIOLENCE

If you are worried that you have a tendency to sexual violence you should try discussing the problem with your doctor who might refer you to:
The Portman Clinic
8 Fitzjohns Avenue
LONDON NW3 5NA
Tel: 071 794 8262

ASSAULT

Rape Crisis Centre

PO Box 69
LONDON WC1X 9NJ
Tel: 071 837 1600 (London Rape Crisis Centre)
(For girls and women)
To find out the telephone number of the rape crisis centre near you:
  ring the London Rape Crisis Centre (the number above)
  look under Rape in the phone book
  ring your local Samaritans (look up Samaritans in the phone book).

The Gay and Lesbian Switchboard

(24 hour switchboard)
Tel: 071 837 7324
For gay men and boys there is no equivalent to the Rape Crisis Centre but help and advice can be obtained from the Gay and Lesbian Switchboard.

For heterosexual men and boys there is no equivalent to the Rape Crisis Centre. Help and advice can be obtained from a counselling organization (see left).

KEEPING SAFE

Your local library should be able to advise you on whether self-defence classes are available in your area. They may be run as adult education classes or by youth clubs, women's groups, residents' associations or police volunteers.

The Suzy Lamplugh Trust

14 East Sheen Avenue
LONDON SW14 8AS
Tel: 081 876 1838
Personal safety courses.

Index

Acknowledgments

Dorling Kindersley and the authors would like to thank:
Sashola Mahoney, Mark Noble and Candida Ross–MacDonald
for help with the text; the young men and women for
being models; Antony Heller, Louise Daly and
Maryann Rogers for production assistance.

Special photography
Antonia Deutsch

Illustration
Coral Mula

Index
Jane Parker

Picture research
Clive Webster and Joanna Thomas

Additional photography
Stephen Bartholomew, Andy Crawford, Tim Ridley,
Hanya Chlala (jacket front)

Picture credits
Comstock: 44, 46;/R. Michael Stuckey 3b
The Image Bank:/Werner Bokelberg 9
Oxford Scientific Films, Mantis Wildlife Films: 70c, 71tl
Pictor International: 30, 40
Science Photo Library: 66, 67; /Andy Walker, Midland
Fertility Services: 71ct, 71b; /CNRI: 71tr; /John Walsh 70b
Telegraph Colour Library: 87; /R. Chapple 32, 37b; /Marco
Polo 33b; /Paul von Stroheim 87
Zefa: 3r, 29, 34, 45, 77; /Norman 2; /Wartenberg 3tl

t=top b=bottom l=left r=right